NUTSHELLS

ENGLISH LEGAL SYSTEM IN A NUTSHELL

FOURTH EDITION

by

PENNY DARBYSHIRE
Ph.D., M.A.
Senior Lecturer in Law, Kingston Law School,
Kingston University

London • Sweet & Maxwell • 1998

Published in 1998 by
Sweet & Maxwell Limited of
100 Avenue Road, Swiss Cottage, London, NW3 3PF
http:/www.smlawpub.co.uk
Computerset by
Wyvern 21 Ltd, Bristol
Printed in England by Clays Ltd, St Ives plc

A CIP Catalogue record
for this book is available
from the British Library

ISBN 0–421–62410–8

CONTENTS

NUTSHELLS

ENGLISH LEGAL SYSTEM IN A NUTSHELL

Other Titles in the Series

AUSTRALIA
LBC Information Services
Sydney

CANADA
Carswell
Toronto • Ontario

NEW ZEALAND
Brookers
Auckland

SINGAPORE AND MALAYSIA
Thomson Information (S.E.) Asia
Singapore

1. INSTITUTIONS

THE COURT STRUCTURE

The most striking points about the English court structure are that:

1. It is not a faultlessly coherent and single, logically developed "system." It grew piecemeal and various parts of it have been reformed and reshaped to suit the perceived needs of the time. The existing structure is so taken for granted, however, that until very recently it seemed almost heretical to question whether we need two levels of criminal courts of first instance and three civil first instance courts, with jurisdictions overlapping.

2. Most civil cases are not heard in the civil courts at all but in one of the major alternative forums which have proliferated in the twentieth century, *i.e.* tribunals and arbitration. Again, the desirability of this element of the status quo has not been the subject of much official attention. The distribution of work between courts and tribunals is a little arbitrary but has not been questioned since the Franks Committee Report.

It has been left to academics to raise the question of whether the popularity of alternatives is not a reflection on the shortcomings of the civil courts and procedure. Recently, however, civil procedure has been heavily criticized. Lawyers and clients readily opt for Alternative Dispute Resolution. instead of the civil courts and, because of the rising costs of legal aid and the courts service, the Lord Chancellor and his predecessor have actively encouraged this.

Criminal Courts

Magistrates' courts. These can be seen as the most important courts as far as the public are concerned because, to most people, being involved in a court case means being dealt with by magistrates. There, almost all criminal cases commence and about 97 per cent are disposed of. Magistrates impose 95 per cent of all sentences.

In Outer London and the provinces, most cases are heard by lay justices, sitting in twos or threes, advised by a justices' clerk or court clerk. In Inner London, most cases are heard by a metropolitan stipendiary magistrate, advised by a clerk. Most London clerks are professionally qualified, although there are over 300 lay justices in Inner London.

Magistrates and their clerks wear ordinary clothes and no wigs and so do the barristers and solicitors appearing before them. Of their criminal case load, about half are road traffic offences, most of which are decided in the absence of the defendant, who may plead guilty by post. Another quarter are "offences triable either way," *i.e.* cases of median seriousness, where the defendant has the option of a Crown Court appearance instead. The rest are other summary offences. Magistrates hear almost all juvenile criminal cases. These are dealt with *in camera* by specialist magistrates in the youth court.

There are over 30,000 magistrates, who sit part-time in around 350 Benches in England and Wales. Many of the very small, rural Benches have been analgamated in the 1990s. Cities such as Manchester and Birmingham may have over 20 courtrooms in use simultaneously. Magistrates' maximum sentencing powers are six months' imprisonment and a £5,000 fine.

Criticisms. 1. It is an accident of history that most cases are dealt with in Inner London by a professional magistrate, advised by a professionally qualified clerk, yet in Outer London and the provinces the same work is done by lay justices who are advised, mostly, by court clerks the majority of whom are not barristers or solicitors.

2. As the lay justices depend on their clerk for legal and practical advice, he may be tempted to interfere in factual or sentencing decisions.

3. Disparity exists in sentencing between magistrates' courts. Magistrates would defend themselves by saying that these are local courts serving local needs so sentencing will vary from town to town.

4. Since criminal cases have been redistributed from the Crown Court, in the Criminal Law Act 1977 and later legislation, magistrates deal with the bulk of criminal cases, including some very serious ones but criminal law and evidence continue to develop as if criminal cases were mostly decided by judge and jury.

The Crown Court. The Crown Court is the criminal court of first instance which deals with the most serious (indictable) offences, as well as some of those triable either way. These together comprise around two to three per cent of all criminal cases. It also has an appellate jurisdiction (see Chapter 5). The drama of jury trial in the Crown Court captures the public imagination and its buildings, furniture, judges and barristers' garb all add to the attraction of a serious criminal trial. The Central Criminal Court ("Old Bailey") is the Crown Court centre which attracts most public attention.

The Crown Court was created by the Courts Act 1971. Note there is one *single* Crown Court, which is divided between around 90 centres throughout England and Wales.

The six circuits, which evolved historically, still exist for administrative purposes. The Crown Court is divided into three tiers, as follows:

First tier High Court judges deal with the most serious offences here, as well as civil High Court cases. Circuit judges, recorders and assistant recorders may also sit here.

Second tier High Court judges, circuit judges, and recorders and assistant recorders deal with criminal cases only.

Third tier Circuit judges, recorders and assistant recorders deal with criminal cases.

Criticisms. 1. The importance of jury trial in the Crown Court is exaggerated (see section on the jury, Chapter 3).

2. Why preserve two criminal courts of first instance? (See below).

The Queen's Bench Division of the High Court. This division features in the criminal court structure because its Divisional Court, consisting of three puisne judges, deals with appeals by way of case stated from the magistrates' court and Crown Court and it exercises supervisory jurisdiction over all inferior courts, *i.e.* reviewing the legality of their proceedings and orders. The division sits centrally in the Strand and in 24 provincial Crown Court centres. Additionally, non-contested QBD cases are heard at many county court centres.

The Court of Appeal (Criminal Division). This was formed in 1966, replacing the Court of Criminal Appeal. For most purposes, the court is composed of three or more Lords Justices and/or puisne judges. Appeals against sentence may be dealt with by two and other applications by one judge. The court hears appeals of both fact and law (see Chapter 5). Until 1997 it sat only in the Royal Courts of Justice in the Strand but Lord Chief Justice Bingham took the Court of Appeal to hear cases in Liverpool and may continue to hear cases in the provinces. Of course, several Courts of Appeal usually sit simultaneously.

The House of Lords (Appellate Committee). The House of Lords' jurisdiction is not confined to the English legal system, in that it also hears appeals from Scotland and Northern Ireland. The minimum number of judges to determine an appeal is three but is normally five. Apart from the Lords of Appeal in Ordinary (Law Lords), ex-Law Lords, ex-Lord Chancellors, ex-judicial Privy Councillors and other ex-superior judges may sit, although they almost never do. Recently, Lord Chancellors have refrained from sitting but Lord Hailsham sat occasionally and Lord Mackay sat several times. The Law Lords do not specialise but, in practice, appeals from Scotland are heard by at least one Scottish Law Lord and Chancery appeals by at least one Chancery judge.

Appeals are heard in a committee room of the House of Lords and the Law Lords wear lounge suits.

The Privy Council (Judicial Committee). This was formed in 1833. It hears appeals from some Commonwealth countries, including republics. It also hears appeals from the General Medical Council and other professional bodies. It comprises the Lord President of the Council, the Lord Chancellor, Law Lords, Privy Councillors and former Councillors who have held high judicial office and Privy Councillors who hold or have held high judicial office in the Commonwealth.

Criticism. The Law Lords, who often provide a battery of barely reconcilable opinions in the House of Lords are forced, when sitting as the Privy Council, to produce one opinion, with one permissible dissent. Some raise the questions as to why they cannot do this, as they sometimes do, when wearing their House of Lords hats, and make life easier for the rest of us, who have to apply their Lordships' opinions.

This argument is countered by Law Lords like Lord Reid, who thought the single Privy Council judgments inferior, being "no more than the highest common factor of all the views." Further, other opponents cite the example of the European Court of Justice which, it is argued, in having to reach one judgment between its 15 judges, produces a bland amalgam which is difficult of application.

The European Court of Justice. The details of the court's powers are dealt with in Chapters 2 and 5. It consists of 15 judges. For the most important cases they all sit together. One peculiar feature, unknown to English law, is the function of the eight advocates general. These are independent individuals from member states, qualified to high judicial office, or equivalent. One sits with the bench in each hearing and may question the parties, delivering an opinion some weeks later. This sets out facts, law and a suggested judgment. There is now a European Court of First Instance whose 15 judges hear staff cases and applications for judicial review and damages.

The ECJ hears:

(a) applications from member states' courts for preliminary rulings under Article 177 EEC (see below);
(b) direct actions against member states or E.C. institutions;
(c) requests for opinions on international law and the EEC Treaty;
(d) tort claims;
(e) actions for judicial review.

The European Court of Human Rights. This court enforces the European Convention on Human Rights, which includes such rights as liberty, security, fair trial, freedom of thought, conscience, assembly, etc., right to life, right not to be subjected to torture or inhuman or degrading treatment, etc. The United Kingdom, being a signatory to the European Convention, has subjected itself to this court's jurisdiction but is not yet bound by its decisions, although the Labour Government has pledged to make it so bound via the Human Rights Bill, currently (1998) progressing through Parliament. The United Kingdom has been taken before the court on many occasions, necessitating amendments in domestic law, *e.g.* with regard to prison correspondence, treatment of prisoners in Northern Ireland, contempt, etc. Students regularly confuse this with the European Court of Justice, an E.U. institution, although the ECHR is quite independent of the E.C.

Civil Courts

The civil court structure includes the House of Lords, ECJ and Privy Council, all of which have been described, in full, above. There is little to say on the CA (Civil Division) which is not said in Chapter 5.

The magistrates' court. This has been described above but it must be remembered that magistrates have a very significant civil case load, the predominant part being family cases. Lay justices who conduct family proceedings are selected from specially trained panels within each Bench, as for the youth court. They are

empowered to make and enforce most orders ancillary or preliminary to a divorce, *e.g.* separation. Magistrates also have a wide jurisdiction under the Children Act 1989 and can, for example, make
adoption and care orders. Their remaining civil jurisdiction
includes such items as council tax enforcement. They also have an
administrative function, licensing (*e.g.* liquor licensing), which is a
remnant of the days when lay justices performed local government
functions.

The county courts. These courts were created in 1846, in response
to criticisms of the predecessors of the High Court: that civil
actions were expensive and inconvenient, being centralised, making
justice inaccessible to ordinary civil litigants. The modern county
courts (around 260) are thus a cheap, locally-based alternative to
the High Court. Their jurisdiction is limited, according to the provisions of the C.L.S.A. 1990 (see below). They are entirely civil and
their case load consists of contract, tort, especially personal injuries, property, divorce and other family matters, bankruptcy, admiralty, equity and race relations, etc. Many county court cases are
claims for debts. Like the magistrates' courts, the county courts
are very significant to the public in terms of their workload.

Small claims in the county court (under £3,000) are dealt with
by a special simple and cheap procedure, unless the parties opt
for the full-blown procedure. Interlocutory undefended matters and
actions for under £5,000 are heard by district judges and the rest
are heard by circuit judges. Solicitors had rights of audience in the
county court even before the C.L.S.A.

Criticisms. See the Civil Justice Review (below).

The High Court.

The High Court is situated in the Royal Courts of Justice (Strand)
and 24 provincial (Crown Court) centres in the six court circuits.

The Queen's Bench Division. This is the largest, generalist division, consisting of the Lord Chief Justice and 64 puisne judges. It
deals with common law, *e.g.* tort, contract, debt and personal injuries. It contains two specialist courts: Admiralty and Commercial.

Divisional Court. This court hears appeals and exercises the
supervisory jurisdiction, judicially reviewing the legality of the
actions of both inferior courts and the executive. In the 1980s,

administrative law (public law) cases have been listed together in the Crown Office List and dealt with by a group of specialist judges within the QBD. Critics say the Crown Office List is the embryo of a new administrative court, as the Commercial Court developed, similarly, from a specialist list. (**Note**: there are also Divisional Courts in the other two High Court divisions.)

The Chancery Division. This is the successor to the Chancellor's court, dispensing equity. Here the Vice-Chancellor and 17 puisne judges hear claims relating to property, trusts, wills, partnerships, revenue, contentious probate and bankruptcies. It includes two specialist courts, Patent and Companies and the Division sits in London and in eight provincial centres.

The Family Division. This was created in 1970. It consists of the President and 16 puisne judges, who hear divorce cases and ancillary matters, and Children Act cases in London and over 50 provincial centres.

Specialist Jurisdictions

The Restrictive Practices Court is independent of the High Court but consists of High Court judges and lay people. It sits rarely and hears cases relating to restrictive practices and fair trading.

The Official Referees' Court takes complex technical or factual cases from the QBD or Chancery, mainly building contracts, which are heard by circuit judges.

The Court of Protection manages the property of those lacking in mental capacity.

Civil Justice Review (1988): Problems Identified in the Distribution of Work between High Court and County Courts

1. Delay at every level in awaiting trial.
2. The cost of litigation was disproportionate to the amount involved, deterring litigants.
3. Too many cases were dealt with at an unnecessarily high level. 30 per cent of High Court personal injury cases led to awards below the county court level. Evidence showed most claims

below £25,000 could be dealt with by the county court. This unimportant work clogged up the High Court and caused the delay.

Civil Justice Review: Main Recommendations on the Division of Work between County Court and High Court— Courts and Legal Services Act 1990

The Civil Justice Review was very effective, in that virtually all its recommendations, listed below, have been effected by the C.L.S.A. 1990 and subsequent rules, from July 1991. In square brackets I note the legal source of each change.

1. The High Court should be confined to:

    (a) public law cases,
    (b) other specialist cases (*e.g.* commercial, admiralty, building contracts),
    (c) general list cases of *importance* (*e.g.* involving fraud or test cases) or *complexity* (on the law or facts or number of parties involved) or *substance* (over £25,000 value) [section 1, C.L.S.A. and High Court and County Courts Jurisdiction Order 1991].

2. There should be a flexible financial band of £25,000–£50,000, within which cases could be tried by either court, depending on the availability of judges and the substance of the cases, and no upper limit on county court jurisdiction [1991 Order and section 3, C.L.S.A. respectively].

3. All personal injury cases should commence in the county court, with discretionary transfer upwards [up to £50,000—1991 Order].

4. Small claims should be increased to £1,000 [C.C. Rules 1991 and since raised to £3,000 in 1996].

5. Generally speaking, the same remedies should be available in both courts [section 3, C.L.S.A.].

6. A plaintiff should be free to commence a case where he chooses [True as to venue: C.C.R. 1991, but not as to level].

7. The Review Body considered but rejected the proposition that there should be one civil court, replacing High Court and county courts, on grounds of "specialist efficiency." Certain specialist cases need to be handled, from the outset, at High Court level by judges with specialist expertise (Judicial review; Anton Piller and Mareva applications).

8. Registrars' jurisdiction should be increased to £5,000 and the High Court work absorbed by the county courts should be dealt with by circuit judges. [Registrars renamed district judges under section 74, C.L.S.A.; jurisdiction increased in 1991 Order].

For further points on the Civil Justice Review, see Chapter 4. If the Woolf recommendations (1996) are implemented, the distinction between High Court and county court will become less significant. The rules will be the same, in the two courts. Complex trials will be concentrated in trial centres.

Distribution of Work between the Criminal Trial Courts

This was reviewed by the James Committee, in 1976, whose report resulted in the Criminal Law Act 1977. They concluded that there were offences which were so serious in the public eye that they should always be triable on indictment "in order to signify the gravity with which society regards them." The 1977 Act redistributed work towards the magistrates' courts and there has been a further increase in the classification of offences as summary, in the Criminal Justice Act 1988 and other legislation.

Court Administration: The Civil Justice Review

The Review's most significant recommendations, in this respect, were:

1. The oversight of administration on the six circuits by the Presiding Judges should be strengthened and the county courts, or groups thereof, should have residing judges.
2. Listing officers, assisted by computer, should be used in all county courts to plan the best use of court time.
3. Management information systems should be enhanced.
4. Courts should aim to sit for five hours, five days per week.
5. The High Court long vacation, now all August and September, should be cut down to August. [Not effected.]

Should There Be One Family Court?

Space precludes the discussion of this live, highly topical and, thus, important issue but the complex current distribution of family cases is discussed in Zander, *Cases and Materials On The English Legal System*. Lord Chancellor Mackay saw the Children Act 1989 as a first step towards the creation of a family court, but no further progress has been made.

ALTERNATIVES TO THE COURTS

This century, some major alternative forums to the courts have been established, providing non-judicial settlement of legal disputes. Lawyers should be concerned to discover to what extent their growth in popularity is a reflection on the inadequacies of the court system.

Tribunals

What are tribunals and how do they compare with courts?
Tribunals are too disparate to be described as a "system." Indeed, there are over 60 sets of tribunals. Their only cohesive element is that many are supervised by the Council on Tribunals. This body has no equivalent in the court system. It deals with day-to-day complaints on tribunal functioning, occasionally inspects proceedings and is consulted on the formulation of new tribunal procedural rules.

Tribunals are highly specialised, each set dealing with only one area of the law. Many deal with disputes between the citizen and the state, *e.g.* over tax or state benefits and others adjudicate between private parties, *e.g.* industrial tribunals.

Some tribunals form a nationwide network (*e.g.* national insurance tribunals), whilst others are a single, central unit. Some sets contain an internal appeal structure, *e.g.* on immigration and industrial relations.

Why have over 60 sets of tribunals developed alongside, but outside, the court system? Most tribunals have been created by statute, this century. As the welfare state grew, so machinery became necessary to adjudicate between citizen and state. The Labour and Liberal Governments which developed state power also distrusted the conservative (Conservative) judiciary, so created tribunals to serve this purpose.

Despite their concern over this creeping bureaucracy, Conservatives never stemmed the growth of tribunals. The Franks Committee was established, to examine their concern, and reported, in 1957, that tribunals should be seen as performing a judicial, not an executive, function and they should be better regulated. Their report led to statutory regulation under the Tribunals and Inquiries Act 1958 (now 1992) and the creation of the Council on Tribunals. The Franks Committee identified four main sets of reasons for the popularity of tribunals:

(i) Cheapness (no formal buildings or judicial regalia, etc.).
(ii) Accessibility and speed.
(iii) Freedom from technicality.
(iv) Expert knowledge (of the panel, compared with a judge, who is a Jack-of-all-trades).

Arbitration

Arbitration is, nowadays, the commercial world's alternative to slow, expensive and inconvenient High Court litigation. It means the settlement of a dispute, usually by an individual expert in the subject-matter involved, or a lawyer. Arbitration may arise in one of three ways:

1. By contract. The parties may have contracted together, in some context, *e.g.* shipping or insurance and, in a clause of their contract, they have agreed to refer any disputes arising under it to an arbitrator (who may be named in the contract). This is significant, not just because it is common trade practice (*e.g.* in standard form building contracts), but also because lay people are often, unwittingly, parties to an arbitration clause. For instance, almost all vehicle insurance policies contain, in the small print, a clause (called a *Scott* v. *Avery* clause) stating that any dispute over a claim will first be referred to an arbitrator, before any court claim may be made. Where one of the parties tries to ignore such a clause, the court in which he makes his claim may order a "stay" (a stop) of proceedings so that the matter may be referred to arbitration.

2. By reference from the court. A judge in the Commercial Court may refer a dispute to an arbitrator.

3. By statute. In certain contexts a dispute must go to arbitration.

The rise of arbitration occurred in the late nineteenth century when trade associations wished to have their disputes settled by experts in their trade. London is an international arbitration centre, dealing with 70 to 80 per cent of the world's maritime arbitrations. The popularity of arbitration now rests on expertise, privacy and finality. Some arbitrations are expensive and fraught with delay, like the High Court. Arbitration is regulated by the Arbitration Act 1996.

Small Claims

In the early 1970s the Consumers' Association and others criticised the county court system for being so cumbersome and expensive as to deter small claimants. Often costs were much higher than the amount claimed. In 1973, the small claims procedure was established in the county courts. All claims of under £3,000 must be referred to arbitration, unless they involve a difficult question of law or an issue of fraud. Procedure is informal but not meant to be a complete departure from the adversarial model. Legal representation is allowed but discouraged by the no-costs rule. The system is, deceptively, called "arbitration" but, unlike arbitration resulting from contract, it remains in the control of the court and the award made is an order of the court.

The Civil Justice Review recommended the automatic small claims procedure be extended to £1,000 (now £3,000) that "small claims" be referred to as such and have their own body of rules and that registrars (now district judges) hearing them should adopt an interventionist role, dispensing with formal rules of evidence and procedure and assuming control of evidence, thus clarifying that their role should be more inquisitorial than in the normal English court. Accordingly, the C.L.S.A. 1990, s.6 clarifies that rules may provide for this.

Alternative Dispute Resolution (A.D.R.)

This is the fashionable development of the 1990s. Many British lawyers, most notably the previous, Conservative Lord Chancellor, are taking an active interest in this American import, as a means of avoiding the public and private expense and the private pain of litigation. Many 1990s bodies have been keen to extend the use of A.D.R.

There are three main categories of scheme: *mediation, conciliation* and *arbitration* (above). Schemes may be private or court-linked.

Mediation is the least formal. The parties voluntarily refer their dispute to an independent third party who will discuss the issues with both sides, normally in separate rooms and, by acting as a "go-between," she will assist them to discuss and negotiate areas of conflict and identify and settle certain issues. The best known of such schemes are those offered to family disputants. Thousands of people, notably solicitors, are being trained as mediators to satisfy the requirements of the Family Law Act 1996. Divorcing couples may be granted legal aid for mediation and may be directed to meet a medicator, starting in 1999.

Conciliation lies midway between informal mediation and formal arbitration. The process is very similar to mediation but the third party may offer a non-binding opinion which *may* lead to a settlement. Many county courts have in-court conciliation schemes and in 1993 a practice statement announced that parties in the QBD Commercial Court would be invited to consider A.D.R., in appropriate cases, such as where the litigation costs would outweigh the amount in dispute.

Arbitration is the most formal (and established) type of A.D.R. (see above). It may be the last resort where conciliation fails. In certain schemes, a conciliator may transform into an arbitrator, where necessary, and pronounce a binding decision.

2. SOURCES

DOMESTIC LEGISLATION

Whilst most principles of English law are derived from common law and equity, most details are now contained in statute law, *i.e.* Acts of Parliament and delegated legislation.

Acts of Parliament

E.C. lawyers would argue that it is no longer a constitutional fundamental that Parliament is sovereign, in that it can legislate whatever it sees fit. Because of the doctrine of subsidiarity, member states can only legislate on matters not covered by the Treaty of Rome. Acts which run counter to E.C. law run the danger of being suspended or declared invalid (*Factortame* (1991), see below). Provided an Act has been passed by both Houses, received royal assent and enrolled on to the parliamentary roll, it cannot be questioned by the courts. The exception to this is where the House of Lords refuses to pass a Bill. Under the Parliament Acts 1911, 1929, it may be overridden and passed by the Commons only (*e.g.* War

Crimes Act 1991). Parliament cannot be bound by its predecessors or bind its successors.

Functions of Acts.

1. Revision of substantive rules of law. The formation of the Law Commission in 1965 has helped keep the law under review and the modernisation and simplification of the law has sometimes been prompted by its reports or those of the Criminal Law Revision Committee or ad hoc Royal Commissions or committees.

2. Consolidation of enactments. Where law has evolved piecemeal, a single replacement Act of Parliament can be passed without debate.

3. Codification. The enacting of rules of common law.

4. Collection of revenue. The annual Finance Act implements the budget.

5. Social legislation. This broad category covers the many facets of the Government's running of the country and organisation of society. It is often the subject of party political differences.

Forms of Acts. Distinguish between (the more common) *public Acts* which are of general effect and *private Acts*, which deal with personal or local matters. Procedure differs.

Distinguish between *Government Bills*, the vast majority, *private bills, hybrid bills* and *private members' Bills*, promoted by M.P.s or peers, selected by ballot. Matters of conscience (*e.g.* abortion) are often left by the Government to be dealt with in this way.

Validity of Acts. Parliamentary sovereignty precludes the courts' questioning Acts of Parliament where there is no conflict with E.C. law and there is no written constitution against which the courts could test their constitutionality, as does the Supreme Court in the United States. The Human Rights Bill, likely to become an Act in 1998, will permit a judge to make a declaration of incompatibility, where he finds an Act to conflict with the European Convention on Human Rights. This will trigger a special fast-track Parliamentary procedure to amend the offending Act.

EUROPEAN COMMUNITIES LEGISLATION

Sources

The European Communities Act (E.C.A.) 1972 provides that any United Kingdom enactment has effect subject to existing "enforceable community rights" so, by implication, parliamentary sovereignty is limited to passing legislation which does not conflict.

Community Treaties established the European Community and are its primary source of law. They are binding on the E.U. institutions and Member States and, in certain circumstances, may create individual rights enforceable in national courts. The fundamental Treaty is the Treaty of Rome 1957.

Article 189 of the E.C. Treaty sets out the following secondary legislative provisions:

1. Regulations have general, binding and direct applicability in all Member States.

2. Directives are binding, as to results to be achieved, upon each Member State to whom they are addressed, but leave form and methods to each Member State.

3. Decisions are binding on those to whom they are addressed.

Applicability and Enforcement

Distinguish between *direct applicability* and *direct effect*. The former concept refers to the fact that all Treaty Articles and all Regulations immediately become part of the law of each Member State. The latter concept is the vehicle through which individuals may assert that, under Community legislation, they have rights which the ECJ will protect and upon which they can rely in national courts.

The question as to whether a piece of legislation has direct effect is determined thus:

(a) Treaty Articles. In the *Van Gend en Loos* case (1963), the plaintiffs needed to know if they could rely on Article 12 of the E.C. Treaty to ignore the Dutch government's increase of import duty. The ECJ, on a reference from the Dutch tribunal, held they could. The Article created individual enforceable rights because:

(i) It was clear and
(ii) it was unconditional.
(iii) Its implementation required no further legislation in Member States so that Member States were not left with any real discretion.

These tests have been applied to test the *direct effectiveness* of Treaty provisions, Regulations and Directives.

(b) Regulations. These have immediate applicability, as part of the law of each Member State. There is no need for further legislation to implement them and they are binding in their entirety and, like Treaty Articles, can be directly effective according to the above criteria.

(c) Directives. Nevertheless, directives may also have an *indirect effect* in that national law may have to be reinterpreted to conform to them. The *Marleasing* case (1990, ECJ) held that national courts are bound by Article 5 EEC to reconcile all national law, pre- or post-dating a directive, in conformity with it. This development has mitigated the results of horizontal direct effect. In *Francovich and Bonifaci v. Italian Republic* (ECJ, 1991), the ECJ decided that an individual could sue the state directly where he had suffered loss as a result of non-implementation of a directive by the Member State.

(d) Decisions. The ECJ has held that these may create individual rights which domestic courts must protect. They have direct applicability and may have direct effect.

Supremacy of Community Law

Under Community law, that law takes precedence over any earlier or later domestic law. In *Costa v. E.N.E.L.* (1964), the Italian government submitted that its national courts were obliged to follow domestic law which conflicted with prior Community law. The ECJ ruled that, in creating a Community with its own legal capacity, "the member states have limited their sovereign rights, albeit within limited fields, and have thus created a body of law which binds both their nationals and themselves."

E.C.A. 1972, s.2 gives effect to Community law in the United Kingdom. Section 3(1) directs the United Kingdom courts to have regard to E.C. law. This includes the principle of supremacy. Where it appears to the English courts that there is inadvertently conflicting English legislation, they will endeavour to give effect to Community law.

The *Factortame* cases of 1990–1991 (on Spanish fishing in United Kingdom waters) illustrate the power and significance of Community law. In 1990, on a reference for a preliminary ruling from the House of Lords, the ECJ opined that a United Kingdom court could suspend the application of any Act of Parliament on the grounds of its alleged incompatibility with E.C. law and that Community law gave the national court the power to grant such interim relief, even though no such power existed in national law. Acting on this reference, the House confirmed that an interim injunction could be granted against the Crown, in such exceptional circumstances, to restrain it from enforcing an Act which, prima facie, contravened E.C. law. The novelty here is the use of an injunction against the Crown since this is, otherwise, impossible.

Subsequently, in 1991, the ECJ indeed ruled that part of the Merchant Shipping Act 1988 ran contrary to the E.C. Treaty. The concept of an Act of Parliament's being declared not to be in conformity with E.C. law came as no news to E.C. lawyers in the United Kingdom, who were swift to point out that we gave up part of our sovereignty in the 1972 Act but Press reaction was jingoistic and scandalised. Present law students cannot afford to be so insular.

STATUTORY INTERPRETATION

The Need for Interpretation

Interpretation of statutes is necessary because Parliament can only be expected to provide a broad legal framework. It is neither practical nor possible to expect a statute to spell out its effect in every set of circumstances, however obscure or complex, to which it will be required to apply. As the meaning of language is, in some instances, in the eye of the beholder, statutory interpretation is an inherently subjective art.

Furthermore, a draft Bill may be altered or added to by Parliament with minimal time for considering any problems of interpretation and it has long been a complaint of parliamentarians and critics alike that the legislative timetable does not allow for this.

Bennion, in his book, *Statute Law*, identified several factors which can cause doubt as to statutory meaning:

1. Ellipsis. This means the deliberate omission of words the drafts-man thinks are implied. This causes no problem provided all the statute's readers realise what is implied.

2. Broad terms. The draftsman uses generic terms, again, deliber-ately, leaving the decision as to what falls into that category to the judge or statute user. For example, does the word "vehicle" cover a child's tricycle and a donkey cart?

3. Politic uncertainty. Ambiguous words may be used deliberately, where a provision is politically controversial or the government lacks clear intent.

4. Unforeseeable developments. Where novel circumstances arise after the passing of an Act.

5. Miscellaneous drafting errors. This includes accidental ambi-guity and even printing errors.

Traditional "Rules" of Statutory Interpretation

The judges do not employ strict rules of interpretation but common approaches have been identified and labelled as such. To a certain extent, judges select which "rule" to use in accordance with the result they seek to achieve in the case before them. Quite often, judges purport, in doing this, to be seeking the "will" or "inten-tion" of Parliament, as if a Parliament of over 600 M.P.s and over 400 regular attenders in the Lords could be said to have a common and identifiable "will." Other judges more blatantly admit, as did Lord Denning, "we fill in the gaps."

1. The Literal Rule. This simple approach involves giving words their ordinary, plain, natural meaning. One might think this such an obvious and straightforward activity it hardly merited being elevated to a "rule" of judicial behaviour but it was a trend of the eighteenth and nineteenth centuries, much stricter than the "mischief rule" (see below), which it supplanted. Some applications of the rule produce absurdity. For example, in *I.R.C. v. Hinchy* (1960), the House of Lords interpreted section 25(3) of the Income Tax Act 1952 which penalised those providing incorrect tax returns with a forfeit of "treble the tax which he ought to be charged under this Act." Although Parliament presumably intended a penalty of treble the unpaid tax, as the interpretation was rectified by immediate legislation, the House, nevertheless, held that a literal interpretation required the respondent to pay treble the whole amount of tax payable by him that year.

2. The Golden Rule. Rather than sanction an absurdity by the application of "the literal rule," judges may apply "the golden rule," permitting themselves to depart from giving words their "ordinary natural meaning." At its simplest, it states that, if words have more than one meaning, the least absurd is to be applied. The "rule" becomes more controversial in its wider sense, that is, that an absurdity must be avoided even if it results from the *only* interpretation. Some judges will take the pragmatic approach of "reinterpreting" the statute with the aim of reaching a common sense meaning, whereas others think this is no business of the judge.

3. The Mischief Rule. This rule is commonly described as the last judicial approach, if the first two "rules" fail to assist interpretation. It is much wider than the other "rules" and concentrates on determining the meaning of words by discovering the aim of the statute: the "mischief" at which the statute was directed.

Under the contextual approach, described below, the aim of the statute is considered as part of the context of the words being interpreted. Many modern judges take this approach from the outset.

The Contextual Approach

Sir Rupert Cross in *Statutory Interpretation* described, in a more sophisticated manner, the judicial approach to statutory interpretation.

Considering the context. In giving words their ordinary or technical meaning or in delimiting broad terms, the judge must take them in their general context of the statute, and in the statute's external context. According to *Att.-Gen. v. Prince Ernest Augustus of Hanover* (HL 1957, "the *Hanover* case") this includes the rest of the statute, the preamble, including the existing state of the law and the factual context, *i.e.* the mischief the statute was intended to remedy. The statute must be read as a whole.

Some judges refer to "a purposive approach," aiming to promote the general legislative purpose of a statute, to avoid, for example, ambiguities which would defeat the purpose of the statute but this can only be done where judges can determine this from internal or external aids to interpretation (see below) and where such an approach is not defeated by presumptions of interpretation.

Modifying statutory language to avoid unreasonableness.

Under this approach, the judge may read in words which are necessarily implied and he has a limited power to add to, alter or ignore statutory words, to prevent a provision from being unintelligible, absurd, unreasonable, unworkable or totally irreconcilable with the rest of the statute. According to case law, this approach should only rarely be necessary if, for example, there is a mistake in drafting leading to an anomaly. There are a number of cases where the words "and" and "or" have been interchanged, to make sense of the statute.

Resorting to Presumptions and Aids to Construction

Internal aids to interpretation.

Judges commonly say that statutes "must be read as a whole." This means that the first resort in interpretation may be found in the wording of the statute itself.

(i) *Other enacting words*. Another section may provide a clue to interpretation and there is often an interpretation section. For example, the Legal Aid Act 1988 defines such words as "advice," "assistance" and "representation."

(ii) *Long title*. This sets out the aims of the Act. It can be as short as two lines, if the Act has one topic, as in the Legal Aid Act, or as long as a page, in a statute with diverse aims, such as the Criminal Justice Act 1988.

(iii) *Preamble*. Modern Acts may not have preambles but some, such as the Legal Aid Act and the Courts and Legal Services Act, set out their purpose in a section. The preamble cannot prevail over clear enacting words.

(iv) *Short title*.

(v) *Headings, side notes and punctuation*. Although not voted on by Parliament, these are acceptable aids.

Rules of Language

(i) *Ejusdem generis*. A general word following a list of particular ones will normally be construed as restricted in scope to applying to things or persons of the same class (*genus*) as those listed; *e.g.* in *Powell v. Kempton Park Racecourse Co.* (HL 1899) it had to be decided whether "house, office, room or other place" included Tattersall's ring at the racecourse. It was held not to be included because "house, office, room" created a *genus* of indoor places so an outdoor racecourse could not fall within an "other place."

(ii) *Noscitur a sociis*. This really means a word is to be construed as being similar to the rest of the objects in a list.

(iii) *Expressio unius exclusio alterus* means that a specified member of a class impliedly excludes other members. For example, the inclusion of "coal mines" in this list: "lands, houses, tithes and coal mines" has been held to impliedly exclude other mines.

External Aids

  (i) Historical setting of the statute.
 (ii) Dictionaries and textbooks.
(iii) Past practice.
 (iv) Related statutes.
  (v) Previous statutes. Consolidating statutes are presumed not to alter the law but clear language may rebut this.
 (vi) Subordinate legislation.
(vii) Government publications (with certain qualifications), *e.g.* Royal Commission or Law Commission reports, Government White Papers.
(viii) Treaties and international conventions.
 (ix) Parliamentary materials. Until 1993, judges declined to refer to *Hansard* but in *Pepper v. Hart* (HL, 1993) the House of Lords held that this rule should be relaxed where legislation was ambiguous or obscure or the literal meaning led to an absurdity and, in identifying the true intention of the legislature, judges could be assisted by clear statements by the Bill's promoter.

Presumptions

(i) General principles. such as the principles of natural justice and the principle that no one should be allowed to profit from their own crime. These override even the clearest language.

(ii) Presumptions ousted by clear words. These are general principles of construction where Parliament must spell out in clear words any intention to avoid the following presumptions:

(a) against ousting the jurisdiction of the courts. The judges guard their own powers jealously and even some of the clearest "ouster" clauses have been held not to preclude judicial review;

(b) against interference with vested rights and that property cannot be taken away without compensation;

(c) against unduly penalising the citizen;

(d) against retrospectiveness;

(e) that statutes do not bind the Crown so that a very common inclusion in an Act is a section specifically binding the Crown (*e.g.* the Royal Family are not exempted from liability for traffic offences); and

(f) that Parliament does not intend to contravene the United Kingdom's international (Treaty) obligations.

The Interpretation of E.C. Law

The most important key to interpretation of Community law is the approach of the European Court of Justice (ECJ). The ECJ is more concerned with examining purpose and context than wording.

The Treaties are drafted in general terms, leaving it to the E.C. institutions, through secondary legislation, to fill in the details. The ECJ can review the legality of acts and omissions of the E.C. institutions.

The ECJ takes a dynamic approach in favour of the aims of the Community and the supremacy of E.C. law over national law, for example giving direct effect to directives. The ECJ employs a "rule of effectiveness" which means that preference should be given to the construction which gives a rule its fullest effect and it takes a contextual approach, referring to the general scheme of the Treaty or other Treaty provisions.

Exceptions to E.C. rules and Treaty obligations are restrictively interpreted, for example the principle of free movement of workers is limited by public policy, public security and public health and these limitations are strictly construed.

The ECJ refers to "general principles of law," common to all Member States, derived from national law and, now, the principles laid down by the European Court of Human Rights, which can be employed in the interpretation of Treaty provisions but which cannot override them. These principles include such things as proportionality, *audi alteram partem*, equality and legal certainty. The general principles of law are now an important source of E.C. law and are used to interpret E.C. treaties and when examining national law for conformity with the treaties, as well as being almost a free standing source of law.

PRECEDENT

Significance

The primary hallmark of substantive law in the English legal system is that so much of it is a creation of the judiciary, through the application and development of case law and precedent. For example, the bulk of the law of tort and contract, as well as important crimes such as murder and common assault are a product of this system and not of Parliament. This distinguishes the English legal system from the codified systems of Europe and elsewhere. Under the system of binding precedent or *stare decisis* (to stand by previous decisions), inferior courts are bound to apply the legal principles set down by superior courts in earlier cases. This provides consistency and predictability and obviously depends on a system of law reporting.

The part of a case which forms the binding precedent is:

(a) a statement of law (as opposed to fact);
(b) which forms part of the *ratio decidendi* (reason for the decision); and
(c) in a court whose decisions are binding.

The *Ratio Decidendi*

The *ratio decidendi* (plural, *rationes decidendi*) has been defined by Sir Rupert Cross, in his seminal work, *Precedent in English Law*, thus: "any rule of law expressly or impliedly treated by the judge as a necessary step in reaching his conclusion, having regard to the line of reasoning adopted by him, or a necessary part of his direction to the jury."

The *ratio decidendi* (*ratio*) must be distinguished from an *obiter dictum* (plural *dicta*) which is a statement of law not necessary for the decision in the case.

A judge may decline or find it difficult to apply the *ratio decidendi* of a previous decision because:

(1) he does not agree with it and has managed to find discrepancies in the instant case which allow him to distinguish it from the precedent; or

(2) no statements of principle appear in the precedent; or

(3) the *ratio* is difficult to extrapolate because different sets of reasoning have been used to found one decision, *e.g.* in House of Lords cases where there appear to be up to five *rationes decidendi* (*e.g. Hyam v. D.P.P.* (1974); *Boys v. Chaplin* (1968)).

Such decisions may be of some academic entertainment but can be a nightmare for practising lawyers and judges of the lower courts and do nothing to enhance certainty and predictability in the law.

The Function of the Court Hierarchy in the System of Precedent

The European Court of Justice. Under section 3(1) of the European Communities Act 1972, decisions of this court are binding in matters of Community law, on all courts up to and including the House of Lords.

The House of Lords. Decisions of the House of Lords are binding on all the courts below it and, until 1966, were binding on later decisions of the House itself. In 1966, however, the Lords of Appeal announced that they no longer intended to be bound by their previous decisions. This new, self-conferred power was intended to be used sparingly, however, to cater for revisions in law necessitated by changing social circumstances. It was such a change in societal attitudes which, arguably, led to the first application of the new power in *British Railways Board v. Herrington* (HL 1972), strengthening tortious protection for child trespassers, when the harsh precedent of *Addie v. Dumbreck* (HL 1929) was overturned. Since then, the House has used this power or consciously declined to use it, on a number of occasions.

The Court of Appeal (Civil Division). The Court of Appeal is bound by House of Lords decisions and its decisions are binding on all those courts below it.

Young v. Bristol Aeroplane Co. Ltd (1944). In this case, the Court of Appeal held itself to be bound by its own previous decisions, with three exceptions, listed (a) to (c) below.

(a) Decisions given *per incuriam* (means: through want of care). This refers to decisions made in ignorance or forgetfulness of some statutory provision or some binding precedent, notably because it has not been brought to the court's attention.

(b) Conflicting decisions of the Court of Appeal. There is no consensus on which of two conflicting decisions, the earlier or the later, should be followed.

(c) Decisions impliedly overruled by the House of Lords.

Later case law added the following exception:

(d) Decisions on interlocutory appeals, *i.e.* decisions taken by a Court of Appeal of only two judges.

Smith & Bailey in *The Modern English Legal System*, list, in addition, the following possible exceptions to *Young v. Bristol Aeroplane*:

(e) Inconsistency with an earlier House of Lords decision: the House of Lords decision is binding.

(f) Inconsistency with a Privy Council decision. This, however, is a dubious creation of Lord Denning M.R.

The House of Lords in *Davis v. Johnson* (1979) reaffirmed the rule that, other than in these cases, the Court of Appeal is bound by its own previous decisions. (See also *Rickards v. Rickards* (CA 1989).)

The Court of Appeal (Criminal Division). This division is bound by the House of Lords, by itself and by its historical predecessors, unless it is a Court of Appeal decision falling into one of the exceptions in *Young v. Bristol Aeroplane*. Additionally, it was laid down in *R. v. Newsome, R. v. Brown* (CA 1970) that a "full court" of five Lords Justices has the power to overrule a previous decision of a court of three.

It is uncertain whether the two divisions of the Court of Appeal bind each other but certainly, in some instances, they have manifested an intention not to be so bound, for example, in their conflicting approach towards the constitutionality of jury vetting in *R. v. Crown Court at Sheffield, ex p. Brownlow* (1980) and *R. v. Mason* (1980).

The High Court. The High Court is, of course, bound by the Court of Appeal and the House of Lords but is not bound by other High Court decisions.

Divisional Courts of the High Court. Divisional Courts, within each division of the High Court are, when exercising their appellate function, binding on their successors and amenable to the principles in *Young v. Bristol Aeroplane* but not when exercising their judicial review function (*R. v. G. Manchester Coroner, ex p. Tal* (1984)).

The Crown Court, magistrates' courts and county court. These decisions are seldom reported and are not binding on any court.

Tribunals. Where a tribunal system has an internal appeal structure, as with industrial tribunals and the Employment Appeal Tribunal, the decisions of the appellate tribunal are binding but tribunals are not binding on each other. Indeed, tribunals are not meant to develop systems of precedent. That is one of the features distinguishing them from courts, even though some tribunals enjoy more than one series of reports of their cases and some tribunals look very much more like courts than others.

Persuasive Precedents

Precedents which are not binding may be taken as persuasive and, indeed, have played a significant part in assisting judicial creativity where there are gaps in the law, a classic example being the development of liability for negligent misstatements resulting in pure economic loss, from an *obiter* statement of the House of Lords. The following precedents are persuasive:

1. *Obiter dicta* of the House of Lords.
2. Decisions of the Privy Council.
3. Decisions from other common law jurisdictions.
4. Textbooks.
5. Judgments of parallel courts, where these are not binding, for example, the High Court.

Law Reporting

Any system of precedent could not function without an efficient system of law reporting and law reporting started privately but somewhat randomly in the thirteenth century but was only put on a formal and more systematic basis in 1870 with the creation of the Incorporated Council of Law Reporting for England and Wales. This body publishes the official *Law Reports* whose contents are preferable in authority to other series of reports, as they are checked and amended by the judges. Nevertheless, they are often practically inconvenient as other reports such as *The Weekly Law Reports* are published so much more quickly.

Databases of both statute and case law, such as *Lexis*, have revolutionised law reporting and the advocate's ability to rely on a broad span of pertinent authorities as they include all decisions, whether reported elsewhere or not.

3. PERSONNEL

LAWYERS

The chief feature of the English legal profession is that it is divided into two sections, solicitors and barristers. The two sides were, traditionally, characterised by their monopolies. The Bar had a monopoly over rights of audience in the higher courts and solicitors have a monopoly over initial contact with most clients. Until recently, solicitors' best-known monopoly was conveyancing. These monopolies have been considerably eroded in the 1980s and 90s and the legal profession has been in a state of flux since it was the subject of scrutiny by the Royal Commission on Legal Services (R.C.L.S.) 1976–1979.

Solicitors

Structure and organisation. On July 31, 1997, there were 91,779 solicitors on the Roll, 71,637 of whom had practising certificates, distributed amongst over 8,842 firms in England and Wales. *The Law Society* is the professional governing body of solicitors, regulating their training, discipline and standards of professional conduct and it is also their trade union.

Complaints and discipline procedure. Since May 1991, all solicitors' firms must have an in-house complaint-handling procedure (although a 1997 Law Society survey found 15 per cent did not have one). Otherwise complaints are processed by the Society itself. The R.C.L.S. heavily criticised the Law Society's handling of complaints. In 1986, the Law Society reorganised their complaints mechanism and created the *Solicitors' Complaints Bureau* now replaced, in 1996, by the Office for the Supervision of Solicitors. Complaints are handled thus: complaints come in from the public and the profession (about 16,000 a year). They may first seek advice from a telephone helpline. The majority of complaints are referred to a conciliator or to a mediator in the Office for Client Relations. At least 30 per cent of complaints are resolved in this way. If conciliation fails, the matter is dealt with formally, with written reports. An assistant director may decide what action to take, with a right of appeal. The O.S.S. has a broad range of powers, including: inspecting the solicitor's accounts; taking control of her files or accounts; or ordering compensation or remission of fees.

It may also prosecute the solicitor before the *Solicitors Disciplinary Tribunal*, which can reprimand, fine, suspend the solicitor or order her to be struck off.

Appeal lies to the High Court or Master of the Rolls. Any complainant not satisfied with the handling of a complaint by the Bureau may complain to the *Legal Services Ombudsman.*

Sex discrimination. The proportion of solicitors holding practising certificates who are women is 32.8 per cent. This reflects a steady growth but it by no means reflects the growth in the proportion of law graduates who are women (around 51 per cent), or women as new trainee solicitors (52.9 per cent), or women of those newly admitted (52.2 per cent).

The Law Society's *Annual Statistical Report* 1997 which provides these statistics also demonstrates how few women are partners. 55.3 per cent of men are partners compared with only 24.8 per cent of women, although the proportion of solicitors, including partners, who are women, is growing.

A 1997 salary survey revealed that female solicitors earn significantly less then their male counterparts, even when all relevant factors, such as experience, are comparable.

Race discrimination. The R.C.L.S. found discrimination in both sides of the profession. It deprecated the formation of firms of solicitors and chambers composed solely of members of ethnic minorities. If black-only firms served black clients and briefed black barristers then the public would come to think such discrimination was reflected in the administration of justice itself.

The Law Society in 1986 belatedly established an ethnic monitoring scheme and a Race Relations Committee to examine complaints of discrimination, consider relevant statistics and work to "enhance awareness in the profession." In 1997, about 4.5 per cent of solicitors with practising certificates were from ethnic minorities, compared with 5.2 per cent of the economically active population. 18.6 per cent of students enrolling with the Law Society are non-white but the biggest problem minorities face is in entering the profession and progressing to partnerships within it. The Law Society's 1994 research report, *Entry into the Legal Professions*, showed minority students experience far more difficulty in securing traineeships than whites. One development by the Legal Aid Board, however, has potential far-reaching effects. A mandatory condition of the granting of a legal aid franchise to a solicitors' firm requires them to demonstrate that they are not discriminating. The threat of a lost franchise and, thus, significant loss of livelihood, may be much more powerful than the fine imposed after a successful complaint to the C.R.E.

Barristers

Structure and organisation. On October 1, 1997 there were 9,369 practising barristers, distributed between 576 sets of chambers, of which 302 were in London, or working as sole practitioners (156). The Bar has grown considerably since 1960, when there were only 1,919.

The General Council of the Bar and of the Inns of Court (known as "*the Bar Council*") is the professional governing body of the Bar. It comprises elected barristers. The Bar Council performs similar professional functions to the Law Society. In addition, the six court circuits have their own Bar Associations, as do specialist barristers.

Further, there are four *Inns of Court*, Gray's Inn, Lincoln's Inn, Inner Temple and Middle Temple and each barrister must belong to an Inn of Court. The Inns, in their (fascinating) history had a collegiate function. Nowadays they own and administer much of the property in which barristers rent accommodation for their chambers (offices).

The Council of Legal Education regulates and provides training.

Complaints and discipline. In 1997, the Bar established a formal system for dealing with complaints, supervised by a Complaints Commissioner. He may award up to £2,000 compensation, with the ultimate sanction being an appearance before the Disciplinary Tribunal, which may reprimand, suspend, disbar and order repayment of fees.

Barristers cannot be sued by their clients for negligence in court or in preparation of court work: *Rondel v. Worsley* (HL 1969) and *Saif Ali v. Sydney Mitchell* (HL 1978) but the opposing client may sue for breach of duty: *Kelly v. L.T.E.* (CA 1982) and the immunity does not extend to negligent advice. Barristers' common law immunity is extended to other advocates by the Courts and Legal Services Act (C.L.S.A.) 1990, s.62 which also provides immunity from breach of contract suits in the same context.

Archaic practising arrangements

1. Chambers. Until 1990 every practising barrister had to rent a "tenancy" (really a sub-tenancy) in a "set" of chambers and until the 1980s most London Chambers had to be within the Inns of Court in accordance with an unwritten rule. The growth of the Bar since the 1960s led to chronic overcrowding in the Inns of Court and by 1990 the Bar Council resolved to abandon all restrictions on the setting up of new chambers. Barristers of three years' call may now practise independently (for example from home).

2. The clerk. Most sets of chambers have one chief clerk and several juniors. All barristers in chambers must obtain their work and negotiate for fees through the medium of the clerk. This is because it was thought unseemly for the gentlemen of the Bar to negotiate with solicitors or tout for their own business. Barristers need clerks as office and business managers and agents. They are often, individually, dependent on them, especially when newly qualified, as the clerk distributes much of the work coming into chambers. Most clerks are paid not a salary but a percentage of their barristers' fees. The R.C.L.S. found clerks earned, on average, more than most barristers. A few sets of chambers have no clerk or have an administrator instead.

3. The hierarchy. The top 10 per cent or so of barristers are called Queen's Counsel, more commonly called "silks," as they are entitled to wear a silk gown instead of the ordinary stuff gown. All other barristers, however elderly, are known as junior barristers or pupils (see below). Q.C.s take the most serious cases and charge high fees.

Q.C.s are appointed by the Crown on the recommendation of the Lord Chancellor. Junior barristers apply to "take silk." Most apply because they wish to specialise in advocacy and have built up a workload and reputation that justifies hiving off some of their preparatory work to junior counsel. There used to be a rule called the Two Counsel Rule whereby a Q.C. had to pay a junior to appear with him in court. This was abolished in 1977, following criticism by the Monopolies and Mergers Commission, but it is still widely followed, in practice. The practice has been the subject of repeated criticism and scrutiny and regulations inspired by the Lord Chancellor's Efficiency Commission on Criminal Practice have made serious inroads into the practice, from November 1988.

4. Partnerships. Barristers stand or fall by their own individual skills (and health). They are not allowed to form partnerships except if practising overseas.

5. Unpaid pupillage. Barristers are qualified as soon as they are "called" on passing the Bar Finals but, if they wish to practise, they must do a one-year apprenticeship, called pupillage. In this, they watch their "pupil-master" in court and are supposed to be trained by him but most of them do some work for him, and are not paid for it. They can earn fees by taking cases on their own account, in their second six months, but having to support themselves in their first six was one of the factors which made going to the Bar so expensive for those who did not have family or other financial backing to maintain them. The Bar has endeavoured to ease this problem by providing pupillage funding (see below).

6. Rules of etiquette and unwritten rules. These seem largely designed to mark out the Bar as an elite, relative to solicitors and clients. They also serve as a good tourist attraction. These are some of the best known:

(a) Barristers never shake hands. The theory is they all know one another. They address one another by surnames, in the old public school tradition.
(b) They use grovelling language to the bench, *e.g.* "may it please your Lordship . . . ," "I humbly submit." Fellow barristers are referred to as "my learned friend," whereas solicitors are simply "my friend."
(c) There are strict rules of dress which require all to wear dark suits and women to look as much as possible like men. Most men wear a waistcoated suit and, under the wig and gown, this garb can be too hot in summer.
(d) Barristers are forbidden from interviewing their clients, other than in the presence of the solicitor.

Sex discrimination. The R.C.L.S. (1979) found that over 90 sets contained no women and some sets of chambers were prepared to admit to a "no women" policy. The proportion of women as practising barristers is nevertheless increasing (24 per cent on October 1, 1997) and, in 1990, the C.L.S.A., s.64 outlawed sex discrimination (see below).

Race discrimination. There have long been complaints by black barristers that racism is institutionalised at the Bar. The R.C.L.S. deprecated the concentration of ethnic minorities into "ghetto" chambers and 10 years later, a 1989 survey showed that half of all chambers had no ethnic minority tenants and 53 per cent of non-white barristers were concentrated in 16 sets of chambers.

Under pressure from the Society of Black Lawyers, the Bar established a Race Relations Committee in 1983. The C.L.S.A. 1990, s.64 illegalised sex and race discrimination by, or in relation to barristers, in terms of offers of pupillage, tenancies and the distribution of work by the clerk and the provision of it (by solicitors), etc.

Amid continuing and widespread allegations of discrimination, the Bar Council established a scheme to twin "ghetto" chambers with white chambers, to allow the former to benefit from the latter's better library facilities and advice and, in 1991, they adopted what *The Independent* described as "the most radical equal opportunities policy of any profession." It proposes that all sets should aim to have five per cent of their tenants from ethnic minorities and that public and private bodies should be encouraged to send five per cent of their legal work to ethnic minority barristers, with the Council publishing an ethnic minority directory to this end.

Nevertheless, a 1993 Bar Council survey revealed the astonishing statistic that only 330 (0.06 per cent) of 5,193 respondent barristers were minority. Considering that about 16 per cent of law students and over 20 per cent of applicants for the Bar Vocational course are minority, the Bar surely has a serious case to answer. In 1993, the Council for Legal Education introduced a central selection Board to review its Bar vocational course selection procedures, as statistics showed white candidates were twice as likely to be admitted as non-whites. At the same time, the Barrow Committee investigated discrepancies between white and minority success rates in the Bar exams. It reported, in April 1994, that even after sophisticated analysis of prior educational achievement, ethnicity was a significant determinant of success, as were offers of a pupillage and achievement of scholarships, in all of which respects white candidates fare better. In 1994 the Commission for Racial Equality conducted a formal investigation into the C.L.E. but, in 1997, there is still a disparity in Bar Finals' pass rates.

The Abolition of the Conveyancing Monopoly

Perhaps the best known professional monopoly was that of solicitors over property conveyancing. It was the main driving force of controversy behind the establishment of the R.C.L.S. Conveyancing had long been known as the "bread-and-butter" fee earner for solicitors. The public complaint was that the monopoly allowed overcharging. Solicitors defended themselves by saying the monopoly protected the public from charlatans.

The R.C.L.S. disappointed all critics by recommending in favour of the monopoly but in 1984, the Farrand Committee recommended a system of licensed conveyancers which was effected by the Administration of Justice Act 1985.

Solicitors perceive the threat of conveyancing by employed solicitors, by banks and building societies, to be much more serious to their livelihood, however. The Building Societies Act 1986 gave the Lord Chancellor power to permit this, although Lord Mackay never exercised it.

Instead, he produced new proposals for legislation regulating conveyancing in one of his famous 1989 pack of three *Green Papers* on reforming legal services. It was entitled *Conveyancing by Authorised Practitioners* (Cm. 572) and proposed to scrap the framework for authorising conveyancing institutions and individuals contained in the Building Societies Act as being too elaborate but, nevertheless, to permit conveyancing by institutions under a simplified framework.

The green paper denied solicitors' allegations that there would be a danger of conflicts of interest in "one-stop shopping" by house buyers obtaining their new home, conveyancing and mortgage under one roof, as lending institutions would only be permitted to do conveyancing by using employed solicitors or licensed conveyancers. Solicitors continued to argue that the public would be insufficiently protected and, worse, that the "unfair competition" from banks and building societies would extinguish most firms of high street solicitors, thus denying the public easy access to legal services.

There swiftly followed the Government's refined plans in the 1989 *White Paper*, entitled *Legal Services: A Framework For the Future* (Cm. 740). They proposed to add further safeguards for the public against conflicts of interest.

The end product, the C.L.S.A. 1990, ss.34–53, provides the regulatory machinery.

Section 17 sets out *the statutory objective and the general principle* of providing for new or better ways of providing legal services (including conveyancing services) and a wider choice of persons providing them.

Sections 34 and 35 establish *The Authorised Conveyancing Practitioners Board*, with the general duty to seek to develop competition in the provision of conveyancing services and to authorise conveyancing practitioners.

Section 41 establishes *conveyancing appeals tribunals* to hear appeals from people aggrieved by the Board's decision.

Section 43 requires the Board to set up a *conveyancing ombudsman scheme* to hear complaints about authorised practitioners.

Repercussions of the Abolition

1. Advertising. The ban on solicitors' advertising was relaxed, in 1984, and further so in 1986 and 1987. Solicitors now advertise on radio, television and in newspapers.

2. Conveyancing costs fell, probably as a result of internal competition (the public habit of "shopping around" rather than remaining faithful to "the family solicitor"). By 1991 some firms started to form networks, preparing to offer attractive conveyancing packages to banks and building societies.

3. Property shops. Solicitors began selling houses, allowing the client to obtain estate agency and conveyancing services under one roof, but numbers of firms selling houses declined dramatically, with the recession, from 1989–1994. There is currently (1997–1998) an attempt to relaunch 12 Solicitors' Property Centres.

4. A Legal Practice Directorate was established, in 1987, by the Law Society to identify areas where solicitors could expand their work. The *Law Society Strategy For The Decade* (1991) emphasises potential new work in: advocacy; A.D.R.; financial services; the single European market; multinational partnerships; networking and specialising in personal injury work, disaster litigation, social security, etc. It has now been re-formed as the *Policy Directorate*.

5. Multi-disciplinary partnerships *i.e.* the possibility of solicitors joining other professional partners, such as accountants, surveyors or tax advisers, was given legal sanction by section 66 of the C.L.S.A. but in 1997–1998 the Law Society is still discussing whether to permit them.

6. International Standards. The Law Society has recently been concerned with launching a scheme whereby solicitors' firms can apply for I.S.O. 9000 for the quality of their services. This is part of their present emphasis on client care and quality.

Abolition of the Probate and Litigation Monopolies

As well as enjoying a monopoly over conveyancing, for most of this century, solicitors have also held monopolies over *probate work* and the *conduct of litigation*, similarly protected by the Solicitors Act. Accordingly, C.L.S.A., s.28. permits appropriate "authorised bodies" (*i.e.* professional bodies, notably the Law Society) to grant the right to conduct litigation, in a broadly similar way to the granting of rights of audience. Sections 54 and 55 of the C.L.S.A. open up probate services to approved banks, building societies, insurance companies and legal executives.

Abolishing the Bar's Monopoly over Rights of Audience

Solicitors have long held a statutory right to appear in magistrates' courts, county courts and (in a very few localities), in the Crown Court. Barristers have enjoyed a customary monopoly, fixed by a committee of judges, over rights of audience in the High Court, the Court of Appeal and the House of Lords. Most significant in terms of the work it provided was their monopoly over the right to appear in most areas of the Crown Court.

In 1984, as an immediate response to the threat to its conveyancing monopoly, the Law Society launched a campaign for rights of audience in all higher courts.

By 1986, they had crystallised details of their campaign in a document called "Lawyers and The Courts: Time for Some Changes." It proposed a new career structure, with every lawyer receiving a common education, and a period in general practice, with all enjoying the same rights of audience in all courts. The Bar would be reserved for specialists, upon completion of further examinations. Direct access to the Bar would be permitted.

This was just the latest in a long series of attacks made by solicitors on the Bar's monopoly. To the Bar's relief, the R.C.L.S. had, in 1979, rejected solicitors' arguments, concluding that such an extension would be against the public interest because:

(i) If solicitors were permitted rights of audience only in the Crown Court, this would destroy the livelihood of new junior barristers, who derived 50 per cent of their income from such work.

(ii) Jury advocacy involves special skills, only to be maintained with practice, which most solicitors could not spare the time to keep up.

(iii) Since it is up to the solicitor, under the present system, to select a barrister, he can make a more informed selection than the client could, left to choose amongst all advocates.

In 1986, in order to take the heat out of their dispute, the two sides of the profession established the Committee on the Future of The Legal Profession (The Marre Committee). It reported in July 1988, recommending that solicitors should have extended rights of audience in the Crown Court and should be eligible for appointment as High Court judges.

Government proposals for change. It soon became clear that the Lord Chancellor, Lord Mackay, was keen to extend the Thatcherite approach to monopolies to the Bar's work. In 1989, he published his three *Green Papers* and his white paper, *Legal Services; A Framework for the Future*, making it clear that the Government view was that the best possible access to legal services was achieved by giving clients the widest possible choice within a free and efficient market. This philosophy was to be applied to the right to appear in court, in the same way as to conveyancing, probate, etc. (see above) and all legal services.

In the main Green Paper, *The Work and Organisation of the Legal Profession* (Cm. 570), the Government set out their views on advocacy. Our adversarial system meant that the court and the client were heavily reliant on the efficient and effective preparation and presentation of a case and the maintenance of high ethical standards. Rights of audience should be restricted to those who are properly trained, experienced and subject to codes of conduct. The basic premise was that satisfaction of those requirements should, alone, be the test for granting rights of audience, not whether an advocate happened to be a barrister or solicitor. Rights of audience would depend on the granting of advocacy certificates by professional bodies, empowered to do so by the Lord Chancellor, following advice from a reconstituted Advisory Committee.

The white paper proposals on rights of audience were enacted in the Courts and Legal Services Act 1990.

Section 27 provides the statutory framework for granting *rights of audience*. It provides that rights to appear can only be granted by the "appropriate authorised body" and *section 28* makes similar provision for the *right to conduct litigation*.

Section 29 requires bodies wishing to be authorised under the Act to apply to the Lord Chancellor. The machinery gives the Lord Chancellor, the Director General of Fair Trading, the Advisory Committee and "designated judges," a role in authorising a new body.

Sections 31 and 32 preserve barristers' and solicitors' existing audience rights and their governing bodies are accordingly deemed authorised bodies under the Act.

Repercussions of the Abolition. As with solicitors, the threat of having to compete for work in an open market has already had an important impact on the Bar. In some respects, it has relaxed a number of its practice rules and has even had to acquaint itself with twentieth century business practice and marketing methods, a real shock to the system for this pre-Dickensian profession:

1. Relaxing advertising rules. Sets of chambers are, since 1991, even listing their members in national newspaper ads, and the bar is providing a new market for P.R. consultants.

2. Devising "A Strategy For the Bar" and promoting new areas of work: for example marketing to those professions who may now access them directly, such as accountants, architects; promoting themselves as specialist advocates and merging chambers to provide stronger units.

3. Relaxing the chambers rule.

4. Permitting direct access to non-practising, employed barristers by their employers' clients. This is important, since there are now nearly as many employed barristers as practising ones.

5. Paying pupils and reforming training.

Other Important Aspects of the C.L.S.A.

1. The statutory objective and the general principle. Section 17 of the statute states that the general objective of this part of the Act is the development of legal services "by making provision for new or better ways of providing such services and a wider choice of persons providing them, while maintaining the proper and efficient administration of justice" and subsection (3) goes on to set out the general principle that rights of audience and litigation should only be determined by reference to education, training and membership of a professional body with an effective set of rules. Most importantly, subsection (3)(c) sets out a *principle of non-discrimination*. It is an explicit version of the Bar's cab-rank rule but, of course, it applies to all advocates.

2. The Advisory Committee. Its membership is set out in section 19 and section 20 charges it with the general duty of advising the Lord Chancellor, having especial regard to the practices of other E.C. Member States and the desirability of equality of opportunity.

3. The Legal Services Ombudsman is created by sections 21–26 to investigate and report on complaints against, broadly speaking, the providers of legal services.

4. Contingency fees which were the subject of an individual green paper, are provided for under section 58 (see Chapter 5).

Life after the Courts and Legal Services Act

By the time of writing, over seven years after the Act came into force, nothing has happened. Licensed conveyancers did not destroy the solicitors' side of the profession, as solicitors of the 1970s shrieked it would, since, by 1998, there are still only only 1000 of them and over 90,000 solicitors.

In 1996, 96 per cent of conveyancy was done by solicitors. Nor have banks and building societies had the chance to pose a threat, since none have yet (1998) been licensed under the Act by the Lord Chancellor. Since the 1990 Act there have been arguments involving solicitors, the Bar, the judiciary and the Crown Prosecution Service over rights of audience. The Law Society can now authorise private practitioners as advocates but by 1998, there are only 494, many of whom do not use their rights of audience. This is hardly likely to destroy the Bar as we know it but, in 1997, the Bar lost their fight to stop Crown Prosecutors being granted rights of audience in guilty pleas in the Crown Court.

What is likely to radically reshape the two sides of the profession are the proposals to alter legal education and training (see below), should they come to fruition.

Fusion

The subject of fusion, *i.e.* whether the two sides of the legal profession should be fused into one, has been a topic of controversy for decades. Many commentators consider the C.L.S.A. will be a large step towards fusion.

Legal Education

Briefly, it is as follows, roughly in line with the recommendations of the Ormrod Committee on Legal Education (1971):

Barristers. All-graduate entry. Non-law graduates and mature students do a one-year Common Professional Examination (the academic stage), then they and law graduates do a one-year Bar Vocational Course. Those wishing to practise must do one year of pupillage. During the first six months, pupils may not earn fees and this had led to hardship in the past. Recently the Bar has promoted a scheme whereby all pupils should be paid, either by their chambers or from a central fund.

Solicitors. Non-law graduates and mature students do the C.P.E. or diploma in law. Then they and law graduates take the Legal Practice Course (one year). All must complete a two-year traineeship before being admitted. All newly admitted solicitors must now undertake continuing education courses.

In 1996, the Lord Chancellor's Advisory Committee on Legal Education and Conduct produced a report suggesting a common 15–18 week training for both sides of the profession followed by a specialist 15–18 week course for solicitors (LPC) or barristers (BVC) and by in-service training as a pupil barrister or trainee solicitor.

A number of proposals for radical change in legal education and admission have been suggested, provoked by an over-production in new lawyers. In 1994, over 6,000 passed their solicitors' examinations, yet fewer than 3,500 training places were available in solicitors' firms, although the situation has eased considerably by 1998. The Bar is facing a similar crisis of over-production of new barristers. In 1996, 1,800 newly qualified barristers competed for 850 pupillages.

JUDGES

The Heads of Division

The Lord Chancellor (Lord Irvine of Lairg L.C.) is the head of the judiciary, President of the Supreme Court and President of the Chancery Division. *If* he sits as a judge, he does so in the House of Lords or Privy Council but this is rare. He effectively selects most judges and has overall responsibility for the court service, legal services, including legal aid and the Law Commission. His executive position makes his role as head of the judiciary controversial. Although appointed by the monarch, he is effectively selected by the Prime Minister, is a member of the Government, and normally a Cabinet Minister so the incumbent changes when the Government changes. He is Speaker of the House of Lords. He thus holds important offices in all three organs of government: legislature, executive and judiciary.

The Lord Chief Justice of England (Lord Bingham L.C.J.) is President of the Court of Appeal (Criminal Division) and head of the Queen's Bench Division of the High Court.

The Master of the Rolls (Lord Woolf M.R.) is the President of the Court of Appeal (Civil Division).

The President of the Family Division (Sir Stephen Brown P.) and the *Vice-Chancellor* (Sir Richard Scott V.C.) who is, effectively, head of the Chancery Division, are *ex officio* members of the Court of Appeal.

Independence

It is a constitutional fundamental that judges are independent, that is, beyond the influence of the executive, apolitical, incorruptible and unbiased. Rules and conventions support this:

1. Superior and circuit judges, but not recorders, are statute barred from being M.P.s.

2. Judicial peers (Lords of Appeal, Lord Chancellor and Heads of Division) refrain from participation in House of Lords political debates although they do speak on law reform.

3. Judges are disqualified, by common law, from dealing with cases in which they have an interest, proprietary or personal.

4. Judges are paid large salaries, supposedly to keep them above corruption, which are calculated by the Top Salaries Review Board and not subject to a vote in Parliament.

Regular use is made of judicial impartiality by appointing them to head inquiries into politically sensitive issues such as Lord Scarman's investigation into the Brixton Riots of 1981, Woolf L.J.'s inquiry into the 1990 prison riots and Sir Richard Scott's inquiry into the Conservative Government's illegal sales of arms to Iraq, reported in 1996.

Judicial Neutrality

Writers such as Griffith in *The Politics of The Judiciary* are, however, less concerned over the previously declared political allegiance of the judiciary than over their narrow political and social class backgrounds and socialisation at the Bar, consciously or unconsciously influencing judges, especially in political cases (*e.g.* in administrative law and in cases involving labour relations, civil liberties, students and immigrants, etc., Griffith and other critics traditionally argued that judges show a significantly "right-wing" approach but this criticism could not be applied to judges of the 1990s, seen by the Conservatives as a radical and outspoken nuisance).

Qualifications

The Courts and Legal Services Act 1990 reformed eligibility for appointment by basing it on rights of audience. Prior to the Act, solicitors of specified standing had been eligible for appointment up to the circuit bench and barristers for all appointments. This had been a source of controversy between the two sides of the profession, solicitors arguing that making them eligible for the High Court would widen the pool of able candidates.

Whilst the C.L.S.A. will ultimately respond to this criticism by making solicitors with rights of audience eligible, there are only three solicitor Hight Court judges, as of 1998 and the Act has been criticised, by the pressure group Justice, in *The Judiciary in England and Wales*, 1992. Practice as an advocate, they argue, does not guarantee the qualities necessary for a good judge and "the strong combative or competitive streak present in many successful advocates is out of place on the bench."

Appointment and Selection

Perhaps the most spectacular breach of the doctrines of the separation of powers and judicial independence is the Lord Chancellor (see above). The selection of all judges is effectively in his gift or his and the Prime Minister's. Lord Chancellors have, occasionally, been accused of party political bias (*e.g.* Lord Halsbury last century) and governments are sometimes accused of rewarding their political supporters.

Lord Hailsham L.C., in 1985, described his method of selecting judges. He said he applied three principles:

   (i) To appoint solely on merit.
  (ii) That no single person's view on a candidate should be regarded as decisive.
 (iii) That candidates should not be appointed to permanent posts until they had proved themselves in a part-time capacity, in an elaborate system of part-time deputy High Court judges and assistant recorders, developed since 1971.

Senior staff gathered factual information from the candidate and opinions from the judiciary and senior members of the profession, who knew the candidate. These, and notes on interviews, were kept on file, the factual information being open to the candidate's inspection.

The convention was that barristers did not apply to be High Court judges. He would review the field of choice, in consultation with the heads of division. (Lord Mackay announced he also consulted the head of the Bar.) It was necessary for candidates to apply to be circuit judges. The Conservative Lord Chancellor, Lord Mackay refused to change this system. He explained it in some detail in *Judicial Appointments*, a booklet available free from the L.C.D.

The Law Society have argued (1991) that the present system of appointment, with its reliance on the appointee's experience as an advocate and existing judges' personal recommendations to the Lord Chancellor, discriminates against women, ethnic minorities and solicitors in general, regardless of the Lord Chancellor's repeated assurances that he is keen to recruit more judges from these groups. Indeed, Lord Mackay expressed this as an open policy in *Judicial Appointments* and, in 1994, he announced new plans designed to encourage more women and ethnic minorities to apply. Nevertheless, in 1996–1997 the Association of Women Barristers has vociferously criticised the appointments system as being biased against women. They consider gender bias to be prevalent in court proceedings.

Groups such as Justice have repeatedly criticised the system of appointment based on the say-so of one person, at that a member of the Government, the Lord Chancellor. This is an anachronism, they argue (1992), stemming from the days when he knew all the candidates. They suggest a Judicial Appointments Commission, independent of the executive, of 13 people, 7 of them lay, which would appoint all judges and supervise their training, career development and standards of performance. Lord Mackay resisted this suggestion, insisting that appointments should still be made by the Lord Chancellor but in 1993 he announced a seven point programme of reform for judicial appointments procedures. It emphasised forecasting and planning the need for judges; preparing job descriptions and particularising the qualities needed; introducing open advertising for judicial appointments below the High Court level; the progressive introduction of competitions for vacancies; further measures to encourage applications from women and ethnic minorities; a more structured basis for consultations with the judiciary and the profession and involving lay people (as advisers only) in the selection process. This plan was fully implemented by 1995. In 1997, the Labour Government announced plans for a Judicial Appointment Commission to draw up a shortlist of candidates for the L.C.'s consideration but retracted these plans, Lord Chancellor Irvine explaining that there is not the time to effect this reform.

Promotion

There is no career judiciary in the English legal system. A circuit judge, for example, does not expect to be "promoted" to the High Court and so on. Career judiciaries are a common pattern elsewhere in Europe, where graduates may choose to train for the judiciary rather than practise and can expect eventual promotion and regrading in the same manner as the civil service. Their judges are consequently much younger, on average, than our judges. In

1992, *Justice* repeated their 1972 suggestion of a structured judicial career path and the Labour Government has promised a "more rational training and career structure".

Social Background

Quite apart from the fact that our judiciary is almost exclusively white and male, much research and comment has been devoted to the narrow social background of the judiciary. The results of most of this are cited by Griffith, demonstrating that at least 75 per cent. of most judicial samples surveyed came from upper or upper middle class families, and attended public school and then Oxford or Cambridge. All surveys, the latest being for the House of Commons Home Affairs Committee, in 1995, indicate that most judges are over 60 years old and the higher the rank, the older the average age. It is sometimes argued that this produces a reactionary and out-of-touch judiciary and thus impinges on judicial independence. For example, some would argue that judges are likely to be more sympathetic with parties appearing before them with whose social background they can identify.

Training

Compared with their European counterparts, who receive lengthy training for their judicial careers, English judges receive very little, or none. The Judicial Studies Board supervises some training for assistant recorders. For example, they are required, before sitting in the Crown Court, to attend a three and a half day seminar on trial and sentence, to visit penal establishments and to sit with a circuit judge for one or two weeks. After three to four years, the recorder will be summoned to attend a three-day seminar with specialist speakers and sentencing exercises. Thereafter she will attend such refresher seminars every five years plus an annual circuit-based sentencing conference. The Royal Commission on Criminal Justice, 1993, recommended that substantially more resources needed to be devoted to judicial training at this level. Civil training is similarly provided for appointees to the county court but there is no specific refresher training save annual one-day seminars on circuit and occasional, optional single-subject seminars.

New High Court judges, however, receive no special training other than the refresher seminars attended by recorders and circuit judges and it is often the case that, at both levels, the appointee's experience as an advocate may be in an entirely different area of law from that applied in his judicial role. For example, a commercial Q.C. may suddenly find himself invited by the Lord Chancellor to sit as a Crown Court recorder, decades after his last involvement with criminal law, or a specialist Q.C. may be appointed as a generalist "Jack-of-all-trades" in the Queen's Bench Division. Furthermore, it is sometimes said, especially by newly appointed judges, that practice as an advocate in the English tradition of adversarial, oral argument is the antithesis of training for the English judge's job, the job of sitting, listening, quietly and impartially, to both sides, without undue interruption.

The traditional objection to judicial training is that it could undermine judicial independence (*Report of the Working Party on Judicial Studies & Information* 1978). In 1993, the Lord Chancellor announced a programme of ethnic minority awareness training, in response to Hood's research demonstrating racism in sentencing.

Removal

It is a corollary of judicial independence and immunity that judges, especially superior ones, have an entrenched security of tenure, first established in the Act of Settlement 1701. Now, under the Supreme Court Act 1981, every Supreme Court judge "shall hold office during good behaviour, subject to a power of removal by Her Majesty, on an address presented to her by both Houses of Parliament" and the only time this procedure has been used since 1701 was in the case of an Irish Admiralty judge in 1830, for embezzlement. Misbehaviour apparently did not include convictions for drink-driving but, in 1994, Lord Mackay announced that, henceforth, it would.

The Lord Chancellor may remove an infirm judge, incapacitated from resigning, under the Supreme Court Act 1981, s.11. Under the Courts Act 1971, s.17, he may remove a circuit judge on the grounds of incapacity or misbehaviour, or failure to comply with his conditions of appointment. Judge Bruce Campbell was so removed in 1983 after his well-publicised convictions for smuggling large quantities of whisky and cigarettes.

Complaints

There are no formal powers of reprimand, short of removal. Those aggrieved tend to write to the Lord Chancellor. There are very few famous cases of judges receiving reprimands from the Lord

Chancellor, usually for abusing their immunity from defamation actions for offensive things said in court (*e.g.* in 1982 when a Judge called a hitch-hiking rape victim "contributorily negligent") or for extra-judicial indiscretion, *e.g.* in 1990, when Judge James Pickles incurred the wrath of Lord Mackay L.C., by calling the Lord Chief Justice "a dinosaur" in a press conference held in a pub. Judges can occasion official displeasure by using the media to broadcast their opinions (*e.g.* Lord Denning during the 1970s and 1980s) but Lord Mackay L.C. has announced a novel policy of encouraging judges to be more publicly outspoken. In 1992, *Justice* suggested that their proposed Judicial Commission should review judicial conduct and consider complaints and, in 1993, the Royal Commission on Criminal Justice suggested a performance appraisal system for judges which the Labour Government has promised to introduce.

MAGISTRATES

Distinguish between *lay justices* (Justices of the Peace) who are not usually legally qualified and who sit in twos and threes, on average one day per fortnight, and *stipendiary magistrates* who are professionally qualified and normally sit alone, full-time. Both types are called magistrates. Their jurisdiction is identical but, through an accident of history, the bulk of the case load in Inner London is heard by stipendiaries while in Outer London and the provinces it is heard by lay justices.

Lay Justices

On January 1, 1997 there were 30,374 lay justices, 15,858 of whom were men. About 2,000 new justices are appointed annually. Most have no legal qualification and all must sit at least 26 days, or 52 half days, per year. Although people do sit as magistrates and assessors in other countries, no legal system is quite so dependent upon lay judges as in England and Wales.

Appointment and selection. They are appointed in the name of the Queen to the Commission of the Peace by the Lord Chancellor or, in the Merseyside area, by the Chancellor of the Duchy of Lancaster. They are selected by 95 Advisory Committees, some of which have sub-committees. The committees consist almost exclusively of magistrates and are normally chaired by the Lord Lieutenant of the county, or, in London, by circuit judges. The Lord Chancellor lists several groups who should not be appointed, *e.g.* police and spouses, traffic wardens, M.P.s, members of the armed forces, those with criminal records, bankrupts and persons whose work would be incompatible with a magistrate's duties. Appointments of those under 30 are extremely rare.

The Lord Chancellor occasionally advertises in the national press for candidates and, in theory, anyone can apply to be a magistrate or nominate another person and the Lord Chancellor is encouraging committees to appoint more of such applicants. Otherwise the many Advisory Committees circulate local political parties and other "established" organisations, inviting them to make recommendations. Burney's research into six Advisory Committees or sub-committees confirmed the belief that they tended to favour candidates who were personally recommended by existing magistrates or who had contributed to the life of the local community through some type of "voluntary work." (Burney, *J.P., Magistrate, Court and Community*, 1979.) Their opinions and attitudes were examined by the Committee in interviews and the tendency was, allegedly, for them to appoint a mirror image of themselves.

Politics and Social Background. Whereas the doctrine of judicial independence ensures that the superior judiciary are above party politics, it has proved impossible to keep it out of the lay magistracy. Many magistrates are local councillors. Indeed, Lord Chancellors have directed Advisory Committees to strive to appoint politically balanced Benches but statistics presented to the House of Commons Home Affairs Committee in 1995 showed magistrates to over-represent Conservatives.

By its very nature, the work pattern of the lay magistrate excludes certain groups of the population and favours others. Some cannot spare the time to sit, *e.g.* those who travel extensively for their work, those who are establishing businesses and those whose promotion chances depend on their visible efforts at work. Mothers of small children, like these groups, tend to be under-represented on the Bench. For some, sitting as a magistrate would cause a financial loss (*e.g.* independent business persons and those who are paid by the hour). J.P.s' loss of earnings allowances are only sufficient to compensate the average to low paid. Groups who can spare the time to sit are over-represented on the Bench (*e.g.* retired persons, teachers and lecturers, top management, housewives with adult children). The over-representation of some of these groups can be exacerbated by the fact that, being readily available, they may sit more often than other magistrates.

The class imbalance of the Bench is a source of continuing concern. The Royal Commission on Justices of the Peace (1948) expressed concern that its statistical survey showed the professions and top management were significantly over-represented on the Bench, with a very low proportion of the waged and research by Hood (1972) and Baldwin (1976) showed that, by then, the imbalance had worsened and had not improved by 1990 (Henham).

Complaints have been made that there are too few members of ethnic minorities on the Bench. The Lord Chancellor, in 1987, acknowledged that the percentage of ethnic minority magistrates on the Bench did not reflect the community as a whole but, despite his recruitment efforts, statistics presented to the House of Commons Home Affairs Committee in 1995 showed that too few minority magistrates are being appointed.

Training. The Lord Chancellor is empowered to prescribe minimum training requirements for lay justices and their training requirement has been significantly strengthened for the 1990s. It is now as follows:

1. Induction course (before sitting). Three hours' instruction at Bench level, including the trial system and human awareness;

six hours' observation in court, including at an outside Bench;

six hours' participatory decision-making exercises;

a one-hour appraisal session by the clerk.

2. Basic training (year one). Twelve hours' training plus visits to a prison and a young offender institution and an introduction to the probation service.

3. Basic training (years one and two). Eight hours' training, possibly arranged as a residential course.

4. Further training (after three years and each three years thereafter). This should include an element of chairmanship training.

5. Special training. For justices appointed to youth court or family panels. (Service in those courts is restricted to such specially trained panels.) In 1997, Lord Irvine announced that, from September 1998, magistrates training will be altered to emphasise learning by sitting in court and to require magistrates to demonstrate they have acquired knowledge and skills.

The take-up rate of voluntary additional training varies enormously, however, from Bench to Bench, dependent on the attitude and policies of the magistrates, their justices' clerk and the magistrates' courts committee.

Removal and disqualification. The Lord Chancellor has power, under the Justices of the Peace Act 1997, to remove a magistrate. Most are removed because they fail to fulfil the required 26 days per year of sittings or because they have moved out of the locality. Justices have been removed for being convicted, for being made bankrupt, for refusing to apply laws they disapproved of and for personal indiscretions.

Additionally, the Lord Chancellor may transfer to the Supplemental List any justice of whom, through age, infirmity or other like cause "it is expedient that he should cease to exercise judicial functions as a justice for that area" or if the justice "declines or neglects to take a proper part in the exercise of those functions" (Justices of the Peace Act 1997, s.8(4)).

Justices are, otherwise, automatically retired on to the Supplemental List at 70 years old. Once on this list, their functions are strictly limited to the non-judicial, for example the authentication of signatures, etc.

Stipendiary Magistrates

Stipendiary, professional magistrates have exactly the same jurisdiction and powers as lay justices. They are lawyers with a seven-year "general qualification" (as defined by the C.L.S.A., s.71), at the time of appointment, which is made on the recommendation of the Lord Chancellor. In 1997, there were 49 in Inner London (called metropolitan stipendiary magistrates) and 40 in the provinces. There is a statutory maximum of 60 and 50 respectively. They are supported by 91 acting stipendiaries. The retiring age is 70, extendable to 72.

Stipendiaries have been appointed in provincial metropolitan areas where the workload is too great for the local lay justices.

Should the Lay Magistracy be Replaced, Nationwide, by Stipendiaries?

The advantages of lay justices are these: 1. Lay involvement in the judicial system (trial by one's peers).

2. They are *very* cheap, compared with professionals, being paid expenses only, which many do not claim. Thousands of experienced lawyers would be needed to supply a nationwide professional magistracy.

3. There is a value, of impartiality, in two or three people taking a decision. It is said that stipendiaries become "case hardened," *i.e.* through over-familiarity with certain offences, their sentencing becoming harsher.

Conversely, it is said stipendiaries have these advantages:
1. They work through the case list more quickly. ·

2. They are better equipped to deal with the increasingly complex and technical range of criminal offences and sentences available.

3. A professional magistracy would bring us into line with the rest of the Western world.

One alternative would be two lay justices and a professional chairman but this might carry the danger that, as human nature would dictate, the lay magistrates would defer to the professional.

Magistrates' Clerks

Both lay justices and stipendiary magistrates are advised and have their courts administered by magistrates' clerks. The chief clerk at each court is called the justices' clerk. A justices' clerk may be in charge of more than one Bench and the nationwide trend of the last two decades has been to amalgamate Benches under one clerkship. In 1998, there were 200 justices' clerks, all professionally qualified. The clerks' staff are, like the justices' clerks, appointed and paid by the magistrates' courts committees.

Of course, since many justices' clerks are in charge of more than one court and since most courts have more than one courtroom in session at a time, the justices' clerk necessarily delegates both administrative and advisory functions to his assistants. The staff whose job includes advising magistrates in court are called court clerks or legal advisers, of whom there are over 1,500, and they need not be professionally qualified. Delegated legislation requires that, if not professionally qualified, court clerks should be law graduates or equivalent, or possess a special clerks' diploma in magisterial law, or be qualified by five years' experience before 1980. A 1995 survey of court clerks' qualifications showed that only under half were professionally qualified. The Minister pronounced, in 1996, that he would not effect a policy of requiring all court clerks to be professionally qualified, contrary to the aims of the Justices' Clerks' Society.

This leads to the curious situation where, in most provincial courtrooms, the court clerk advising the lay justices is not professionally qualified. More anomalous is the fact that in Inner London, where most cases are heard by metropolitan stipendiary magistrates, they are usually advised by clerks who are professionally qualified. (Additionally, there are some court clerks in Inner London.)

The nationwide situation remains patchy, dependent on whether the local magistrates' courts committees pursues a policy of recruiting professionals.

The legal position of the clerks in their advisory role is even odder. See Chapter 4.

TRIBUNAL MEMBERS

Chairmen of tribunals are most commonly members of the legal profession, sitting as part-timers. Lawyer-chairmen were favoured by the Franks Committee in 1957 and the reasons are obvious: legal expertise to regulate procedure and evidence and to interpret the applicable substantive law. The other two who sit with the chairman are seldom legally qualified but are selected, instead, to import an element of expertise into the adjudication. For example, the industrial tribunals' members are usually drawn from employers' and employees' organisations; those tribunals concerned with the collection of revenue often appoint accountants and ex-tax inspectors.

Tribunal chairmen are appointed by the Lord Chancellor or selected by the relevant government department or tribunal President from a panel appointed by the Lord Chancellor. Other tribunal members are appointed by the relevant government department, by the Crown or the Lord Chancellor. In many instances, appointments are for three years, renewable, and members are removable by the relevant Minister, with the Lord Chancellor's consent.

The big tribunals, such as the Lands Tribunal or the Employment Appeal Tribunal, need full-time appointees and these are usually of similar status and salary to puisne judges.

THE JURY

Most of what is said in this section relates to trial by jury in the Crown Court, where most juries sit. Juries are also used in coroners' courts and in the civil courts but their use is rare in the latter (see below).

Eligibility

Historically, the jury were the equivalent of today's witnesses, local people who knew something of the defendant or the alleged incident. From the nineteenth century, jury service was confined to owners of property over a certain value. Eventually, all householders became eligible and now the property qualification has been abolished and jury selection is laid down in the Juries Act 1974, as amended by the Criminal Justice Act 1988 and the Criminal Justice and Public Order Act 1994. Those eligible are people on the electoral register, aged 18–70, who have lived in the United Kingdom for five years. Nowhere in the Act does it specify that selection should be random. Indeed Schedule I significantly qualifies randomness by listing those who are ineligible, disqualified or excusable.

Ineligible. The judiciary, legal profession, others concerned with the administration of justice, the mentally ill, the clergy.

Disqualified (as amended by the Juries Disqualification Act 1984).
   Those who have ever been sentenced to custody for five or more years and those who, in the last 10 years, have received any prison, borstal, youth custody or suspended sentence or community service order, or who have been placed on probation in the last five years. Those on bail are also disqualified (C.J.P.O. Act 1994).

Excusable as of right. M.P.s and peers, members of the armed forces, medical and similar professions. The Criminal Justice Act 1988 added those over 65 and the C.J.P.O. Act 1994 added members of religious bodies with beliefs or tenets incompatible with jury service.

Discretionary excusal. Section 9(2) of the 1974 Act permits further inroads into randomness by allowing the jury summoning officers to accept excuses from other individuals for good reasons. What is acceptable is, of course, highly subjective. Thus, for example, Baldwin and McConville found in their research published in *Jury Trials* (1979) that, in Birmingham, excuses were readily accepted from mothers of small children, distorting the gender balance. The Criminal Justice Act 1988 gave summoning officers an additional power of discretionary deferral which should lessen the distorting effects of excusal on the overall pattern of jury selection. In 1988, the Lord Chief Justice issued a Practice Direction guiding courts in excusing jurors. Reasons include personal involvement in a case, personal hardship and conscientious objection. Additionally, judges may discharge those who are incapacitated through physical disability (C.J.P.O. Act 1994).

Selection

Selection from the electoral register is done randomly. At this stage, there are several factors destroying randomness. Most obviously, the electoral register is not accurately representative of the population because of population mobility, house moves, death, and, latterly, because of people declining to register, in an attempt to evade council tax. It is up to the summoning officer which electoral registers he uses and thus which area the jurors will come from. In the 1980s, there were complaints from black defendants that jurors were summoned from white areas. Judges have resisted most attempts to artificially construct mixed race juries but in one trial the judge ordered an adjournment and, in another, ordered a jury to be summoned from a different district, in the hope of selecting a mixed jury.

The group summoned to attend at a particular Crown Court location is called "the panel," from which juries are selected for trials over a certain period (usually two weeks) and the prosecution at this stage may exercise a problematic form of scrutiny known as "vetting."

Vetting

In 1980, the two divisions of the Court of Appeal gave conflicting rulings on the legality of jury vetting. In *R. v. Sheffield Crown Court, ex p. Brownlow*, the Civil Division, led by Lord Denning, unanimously ruled jury vetting by the police to be unconstitutional, although they appeared to accept vetting sanctioned by the Attorney-General using his prerogative power.

The case was closely followed, in the Criminal Division, by *R. v. Mason*, in which police vetting had taken place, although had not been sanctioned by the judge. The Court held vetting practice was supportable as common sense.

In response, the Attorney-General amended the guidelines immediately, enhancing controls over vetting and distinguishing between (a) vetting carried out by the police and (b) "authorised checks," requiring his personal consent:

(a) Police may make checks against criminal records, following guidelines set down by the Association of Chief Police Officers, to establish that jurors are not disqualified.

(b) "Authorised checks" are now to be carried out only with the Attorney-General's permission, following a recommendation by the D.P.P. The D.P.P. decides what part of the information disclosed should be forwarded to the prosecution (**Note**: *not* the defence). Except in terrorism cases, such checks will not now be carried out in politically motivated cases, or those involving criminal gangs and in, for example, Official Secrets trials, vetting will only be permitted where national security is involved and the hearing is likely to be *in camera*.

(c) Additionally, in cases falling under the guidelines, after an "authorised check," the Attorney-General will consider and, in other cases, the Chief Constable may consider, defence requests for information revealed on jurors.

Challenges to the Array

Once the panel has been assembled, all parties have a common law right, preserved by section 12(6) of the Juries Act 1974, to challenge the whole panel, on the grounds that the summoning officer is biased or has acted improperly, *e.g.* this was attempted in *Danvers* (Crown Court, 1982) by a black defendant, on the grounds that the all-white jury did not reflect the ethnic composition of the community.

Challenge by the Prosecution

Whether or not checks have been made on the panel, the prosecution may exclude any of them from a particular jury by asking them to "stand by for the Crown" without reasons, until the whole panel, except for the last 12, is exhausted. Reasons, "cause," must be given for any further challenges but, with panels often consisting of 100 or more, the prosecution rarely needs to explain its challenges.

The Attorney-General announced, in 1988, that the prosecution's right to stand a juror by without giving reasons would now be limited to two instances:

(i) to remove a "manifestly unsuitable" juror;

(ii) to remove a juror in a terrorist or security trial where the Attorney-General has authorised vetting.

This goes some way towards responding to complaints over the imbalance between prosecution and defence rights of challenge.

Challenges by the Defence

Once the jury are assembled in court, the defence may challenge any number of potential jurors *for cause* (*i.e.* good reason acceptable to the judge) but what is an acceptable "cause" has been qualified by a 1973 Practice Note issued by the Lord Chief Justice, who stated it was contrary to established practice for jurors to be excused on grounds such as race, religion, political beliefs or occupation.

It is also clear that the reasons must be those known to the defence and should not normally be ascertained by examining the potential juror in court. In other words, no practice exists such as the "voir dire" system in the United States, where potential jurors are examined by psychologists and other professionals to discover any prejudices. There have been occasional, well publicised exceptions, however, in the 1980s, where the judge has permitted examination of jurors on their affiliations or beliefs, notably in cases involving black defendants.

Until recently, the defence could make a certain number of *peremptory challenges*, that is, challenges without reasons. This has now been abolished, amidst great controversy, by the Criminal Justice Act 1988. This resulted from unsupported but widespread public allegations that the right to peremptory challenge was being abused by defence lawyers, deliberately trying to skew the jury and the recommendation of the Roskill Committee on fraud trials (1986) that it be abolished. This leaves a gross imbalance between prosecution and defence rights of challenge, which the Criminal Bar Association argued was a breach of Article 6 of the European Convention on Human Rights.

Excusal by the Judge

Under the Juries Act, s.10, the judge may discharge from service any juror about whom there is doubt as to "his capacity to act effectively as a juror" because of physical disability or insufficient understanding of English. Additionally, judges have a common law discretion to discharge jurors and they occasionally interpret this quite broadly.

Controversies Surrounding the Jury

There is an ongoing debate between civil libertarians and others about the pros and cons of retaining the jury and jury equity.

Should the jury be retained and does it inject layman's "equity" into the legal system?

PRO (a) The jury rouses strong emotions and seems to be defended by some historians, civil libertarians, politicians, judges and laypeople as the last bastion of civil liberties. For example, Lord Devlin hailed it as a guardian of democracy: "the lamp that shows that freedom lives" and Blackstone called the jury "the glory of English law ... the liberties of England cannot but subsist so long as this palladium remains sacred and inviolate" (*Commentaries*, 1768).

It is argued that the jury acts as a check on officialdom, on the judge's power, and a protector against unjust or oppressive prosecution, injecting jury "equity" by deciding guilt or innocence according to a feeling of justice rather than by applying known law to facts proven beyond reasonable doubt.

(b) Additionally, jury supporters argue that a decision by 12 lay people is fairer than one by a judge alone, since it is likely that 12 people will cancel out one another's prejudices.

CON (a) The importance of the jury system is overrated, for example, when given the choice, being charged with a criminal offence "triable either way," the vast majority of defendants choose to appear before magistrates (source: *Annual Criminal Statistics*) and, of the remainder, who opt for the Crown Court, about three-quarters plead guilty and thus are not tried by jury but just sentenced by the judge. Thanks to this and the downgrading of offences as summary, under one per cent of defendants are now tried by jury (Source: *Criminal Statistics*).

(b) The rate of use of civil juries has declined massively since the nineteenth century. The Administration of Justice (Miscellaneous Provisions) Act 1933 imposed limits on the use of civil jury trial, which remains a right only in cases of libel, slander, malicious prosecution, false imprisonment and fraud but, under the Supreme Court Act 1981, the court can refuse jury trial.

(c) By now, civil juries are rarely used (under 400 trials per year) and examining the reasons why people do not opt for them gives an idea of the drawbacks of jury trial:

The Faulks Committee (1974) recommended that juries should no longer be available as of right in defamation actions because, *inter alia*:

(i) Judges were not as remote from real life as popularly supposed.
(ii) Judges gave reasons, whereas juries did not.
(iii) Juries found complex cases difficult.
(iv) Juries were unpredictable.
(v) Juries were expensive (jury trial is more time consuming, as explanations have to be geared for them, not a judge).

Additional reasons given by the anti-jury lobby for the unpopularity of civil juries are:

(vi) They seldom take notes, are not encouraged to do so, and may not be able to remember all the evidence, thus they are likely to be swayed in the jury room by the more dominant characters' interpretation or recollection of events and to be more vulnerable to persuasive rhetoric than a judge.

Their difficulty in understanding evidence is most acute in fraud trials and was considered by the Roskill Committee on Fraud Trials in 1986. Fraud trials are notoriously long (often over 100 days), expensive and highly complicated.

The Committee recommended the jury be abolished in complex criminal fraud cases and be replaced by a Fraud Trials Tribunal of a judge and two lay members with, where appropriate, a knowledge of accountancy and bookkeeping. Calls for the jury's replacement in serious fraud trials have been renewed since the costly Maxwell brothers' trial in 1995–1996.

(d) The notion that the jury applies its own equity has no substance, Baldwin & McConville in *Jury Trials* (1979) found no evidence that juries acquitted people in the face of unjust prosecution. On the contrary, perverse verdicts occurred at random. The jury thus had the disadvantage of being unpredictable.

---

4. THE ADVERSARIAL PROCESS

The type of litigation which is characteristic of the common law, called the adversarial process, sets the two parties up against each other, as if they were opponents in battle. Essentially, the parties are viewed as equally matched opponents, responsible for preparing their own side of the case and finding their own witnesses and evidence, with little or no involvement by the court. The function of the judge is to hear both sides and pass judgment. It is not to control the gathering of evidence or to dictate the issues, nor to try to effect a settlement between the parties. This contrasts dramatically with many foreign jurisdictions, both European and common law.

Civil Litigation

Pre-trial civil litigation is, not surprisingly, often described in the terminology of a battle or game. Students should be concerned with the question of whether this battle or game model serves private needs and the public interest. There are several points which suggest that it may not:

1. Settlement. The vast majority of civil cases are settled out of court, trial being the "ultimate weapon" in the battle. Of those cases where proceedings are commenced, only a tiny percentage come to trial, the others having been settled or having been given judgment in default of a defence. These represent the tip of a much greater iceberg, as the great bulk of civil disputes are settled even before proceedings have been commenced.

2. Unfairness. The battle analogy presumes the sides are equally matched in terms of evidence and resources but, looking at the litigators, this is not so.

3. Unsuitability. At last, it has been acknowledged that the battle analogy is inappropriate in the context of family breakdown and the Family Law Act 1996 provides a statutory mediation scheme.

4. Delay. This seems to be historically endemic to the English adversarial system and has long ago reached unacceptable proportions. It was the main concern of the Civil Justice Review 1988.

5. Cost. This is another major off-putting feature of litigation.
  The 1988 Civil Justice Review was the most important source, commentary and critique on civil litigation but even since the Review and the C.L.S.A. 1990, yet more review bodies have reported: *Civil Justice on Trial—The Case For Change* (1993) by The

Bar Council and Law Society (The Heilbron Report and the Woolf Report (1996)). This section examines each stage of civil pre-trial procedure and proposals for reform:

Settlement

Proportion. Statistics calculating percentage settlement are not kept but it is possible to estimate the number of settlements in personal injury cases, from the Judicial Statistics and various studies. Less than 10 per cent of those where a writ is issued reach the court door, where a large number are settled. Even of trials which commence, a large number are settled. Further, an Oxford study found that in its sample of 1,711 personal injury cases, only five cases (0.2 per cent) ended up with damages obtained by a court hearing.

Reasons. The pressures on a litigant to settle or even abandon his claim, especially in personal injury cases, are well documented:

(i) Delay. A plaintiff may be ground into submission by strain, uncertainty and the need for compensation if he is rendered workless and disabled by injury. The Civil Justice Review found that, in 65 per cent of personal injury cases, proceedings had not been commenced within one year of the incident.
(ii) Cost and fear of legal fees.
(iii) Payment into court (see below).
(iv) Difficulties in obtaining evidence and the risk of not proving the case.

Generally speaking, the monetary level of settlements is lower than damages awarded by courts. It may be argued that the above factors assert unfair pressure on the plaintiff to settle for a low sum.

Privilege. Letters between the parties (usually between solicitors) to negotiate a settlement are often headed WITHOUT PREJUDICE. This provides a privilege which prevents statements therein being relied on as admissions in any later litigation.

High Court or County Court?

Following the recommendations of the Civil Justice Review, civil work has been significantly redistributed down to the county courts (see Chapter 1) by the Courts and Legal Services Act 1990 and

delegated legislation made in 1991. At present the distribution is
as follows:

The county court should try:

— any action worth less than £25,000 unless the court considers,
  under the new criteria, that it should be tried in the High
  Court;
— all personal injury claims under £50,000;
— equity and probate proceedings under £30,000.

The High Court should try:

— any action over £50,000 (£100,000 in London) unless the court
  decides that, under the new criteria, it should be tried in the
  county court;
— applications for judicial review;
— applications for *Anton Piller* orders/*Mareva* injunctions.

Either court may try actions in the £25,000–£50,000 range, which
should be allocated according to the new criteria.

The new criteria:

  a. the financial substance of the action;
  b. the importance of the action, especially whether it raises
     issues relevant to outsiders, or of general public interest;
  c. the complexity of the facts, legal issues, remedies or pro-
     cedures involved;
  d. whether a transfer is likely to result in a more speedy trial
     of the action.

Parties who bring proceedings in the High Court which the court
considers should have been brought in the county court may suffer
a costs penalty, under the C.L.S.A., s.4.

Commencing an Action

In the High Court, proceedings are commenced by writ, originating
summons, originating motion or petition. Procedure by originating
summons is simpler and cheaper than by writ and does not involve
pleadings.

   In the county court, proceedings between parties are commenced by summons. The Civil Justice Review Body and the Heilbron Report recommended that all proceedings be commenced in the same way as did Lord Woolf (1996).

Summary Judgment and Judgment in Default

If, after the defendant acknowledges service, the plaintiff in the High Court still considers there is no proper defence, he may apply to the master under RSC, Order 14 for summary judgment. In the county court most defendants issue default summonses whereby, if the defendant does not, within 14 days, send in a defence, counter-claim or admission, or the amount claimed plus costs, the plaintiff can get judgment for the full amount, after proving service. Since 1990, defendants can rely on the claim's being automatically struck out if the plaintiff (in the county court) does not request a trial date within fifteen months of the close of pleadings.

Summary judgments and those by default are very significant numerically. For instance, the Civil Justice Review shows that in 1986 there were 2,260 trials in the QBD but 94,990 judgments by default. This is the commonest method of disposal in both the High Court and the county court.

Pleadings

These are formal statements outlining the parties' allegations against one another. Pleadings are a broad outline containing the material facts without detailed evidence or argument. Their significance is that a party must keep to his case, as contained in the pleadings, unless given permission to vary them by the court. The Civil Justice Review said they should be more informative and parties have been so instructed since 1990. The process is as follows: the plaintiff enters his *statement of claim*. The defendant may request *further and better particulars of claim* and must enter his *defence*. The plaintiff may then request *further and better particulars of defence*. The defendant may enter a *counterclaim*. Then the plaintiff may enter a *reply* to the defence and a *defence* to any counterclaim and this performance may be protracted.

Pleadings are closed 14 days after the issue of the last one.

Discovery (Disclosure)

This is now automatic, after pleadings, in the High Court and, since 1990, in the county court. It means that each party must make relevant documents available to the other side, to inspect and copy.

Inspection may be denied one party if the other can show legal professional privilege (solicitor/client communications) or public interest immunity (usually information possessed by the Government) but the documents' existence must be disclosed. The Heilbron Report asserted that much of the cost of litigation was caused by discovery, rendering both pleadings and trial unduly complex and lengthy. They recommended stricter party and court control and enforcement of existing rules to keep discovery to the necessary minimum. They also recommended a pilot scheme of examination of witnesses for oral discovery.

Mareva Injunction

The plaintiff can ask for one of these injunctions, named after a case, to stop the defendant transferring his assets abroad or disposing of them, to prevent himself being able to satisfy judgment.

Anton Piller Orders

Again named after a case, this order allows the plaintiff to enter the defendant's premises to search for evidence.

Exchange of Witness Statements

Traditionally, court rules and the law have not enforced the exchange of witness statements pre-trial. Names of witnesses were not part of discovery. This has often been called "trial by ambush" with each party aiming to keep as much from the other as possible, hoping to profit from the element of surprise.

Our system is commonly compared with the American system where the parties can enforce *anyone*, not just the opposing party, to disclose relevant facts and documents. Anyone may be examined and all witnesses must disclose details of all other witnesses known to them.

Following the recommendations of the Winn Committee, exchange of expert witness statements was introduced in 1974 and the procedure was extended, in 1986, to the specialist High Court sections.

The Civil Justice Review recommended that this rule be applied to most High Court and county court trials. Their reasons were these:

(i) This rule would provide the basis for earlier, better informed settlements.

(ii) It should improve pre-trial preparation.

(iii) It should shorten trials by helping to identify issues and reduce the need for oral evidence.

Since the Review, in 1988, the power to order exchange of witness statements has been extended to all cases in the QBD and the C.L.S.A., s.5 provides a specific rule-making power to require exchange in all civil proceedings.

The Summons for Directions and Pre-Trial Review

In the High Court, with certain exceptions, the plaintiff then takes out a "summons for directions" to bring the matter before a master, to direct the future course of the action. This meeting may indicate that certain points are no longer in issue.

The county court equivalent is the pre-trial review. These reviews are often used to give judgment for the plaintiff where the defendant fails to appear or provides no real defence. The district judge is instructed to make necessary directions in the same way as a master and to "endeavour to secure that the parties make all such admissions and agreements as ought reasonably to be made" (County Court Rules).

The overwhelming evidence before the Civil Justice Review Board was that summons for directions was by now a waste of time since important orders such as discovery are now automatic. The Heilbron Report suggested this procedure was an opportunity for judicial case management and for considering reference to A.D.R.

The Review board recommended that in most cases there should be a pre-trial hearing immediately before trial, which would, in major cases, be conducted by the trial judge himself. Its function would be to determine the trial agenda, issues, evidence and points of law, etc.

This proposed pre-trial hearing was not envisaged by the Review as the opportunity for a settlement. Indeed, like the Winn Committee before them, they specifically contemplated but rejected the introduction of settlement conferences on the lines of those in the United States, where the judge, with the parties, actively explores the opportunity for a settlement.

Payment into Court

If civil litigation can be seen as a game, this is a game of bluff *par excellence*, when the defendant, at any time pre-trial, may force the plaintiff to take a gamble. Where the defendant feels he may lose the case, he offers the plaintiff a sum lower than the damages likely to be awarded and pays it into court. The plaintiff then has to choose whether to settle for the sum paid in or take the heavy risk of pursuing the case to trial where, if the judge awards him the same or less than the payment in, he is penalised by paying all costs from the date of the payment. The judge knows nothing of the payment in, lest the parties suspect the judge of acting on this knowledge.

Payment in has been the subject of repeated criticism that it is unfair on the plaintiff, but the Civil Justice Review recommended no change.

Curing Delay

In the 1980s, the judges themselves, especially the Master of the Rolls, repeatedly expressed disquiet over delay and Queen's Bench delays were reduced, by 1988, from 13 months to three months as a result of allowing strict judicial control of listing. The Civil Justice Review proposed a system of interventionist court control of case progress, as suggested by the Cantley Committee, with time limits, reminders being sent to solicitors and a penalty of striking out for non-compliance. This would make a significant move towards judicial interventionism to a degree unknown, so far, to the English legal system.

More Civil Justice Reform

No sooner had the dust settled over the civil courts, following the Civil Justice Review and the C.L.S.A. 1990 than the Heilbron Report was published (1993). This is not a Government document but that of a group of practising lawyers. It may not, therefore, be as influential as the Review but it prompted the Lord Chancellor to ask Lord Woolf to review civil procedural rules and massively reduce them.

Access to Justice, "The Woolf Report", 1996

Defects identified by Lord Woolf are costs, which often exceed the claim, inequality between powerful and under-resources litigants; uncertainty, incomprehensibility, fragmentation, with no one responsible overall for civil justice and over-adversarialism, with parties running the cases and ignoring court rules. He recommended case management by the courts determining and enforcing realistic timetables and suitable procedures. Defended cases will be allocated to one of three tracks:

- small claims up to £3,000;
- a fast track for straightforward claims up to £10,000, with strict procedures, fixed timetables (20–30 weeks to trial) and fixed costs:
- a multi-track for cases over £10,000, with management by judicial teams of the heaviest cases.

The second stage of his inquiry concentrated on medical negligence, housing cases and multi-party actions, where he felt the system failed most conspicuously to meet the needs of litigants. Lord Woolf was concerned to improve access to justice for small business. He drafted a new set of unified rules for the High Court and county court. His "new landscape" has the following features:

- Litigation will be a last resort, with A.D.R. and settlement promoted.
- Litigation will be less adversarial, with an expectation of openness and cooperation and use of single, court appointed experts.
- Simplified procedure with all proceedings commenced by claim and discovery restricted.
- All cases timetabled (including trial length) and monitored by the court.
- Litigation will be more affordable, predictable (fixed costs in fast track).
- Parties of limited means (unrepresented) will be able to litigate on a more equal footing, with advice services from the courts (leaflets, videos, help lines and IT). Judicial case management will ensure wealthier parties cannot gain tactical advantage.
- A Head of Civil Justice will have overall responsibility (Sir Richard Scott V.C. was appointed in January 1996).
- Judges and courts will be deployed to meet the needs of litigants, with heavier cases heard at trial centres with specialist judges.
- Judges will be given case management training and encouraged to specialise in such areas as housing and medical negligence.
- Legal aid reform must take account of his recommendations

(*e.g.* by providing aid for A.D.R. and funding for court advice services and by recognising the importance of small firms of solicitors, especially in remote areas).

- All recommendations of the Civil Justice Review on providing advice, information and assistance to litigants should be implemented. This is aided by Lord Mackay's creation of the Court Service Agency, with its emphasis on customer service.

Criticisms

The law journals of 1995–1998 contain too much comment to summarise here but the best known are these:

- Many have doubted the capabilities of English judges to effect hands on case management, as they have been required to do the opposite, *i.e.* be non-interfering, during their careers.
- Judicial case management will provoke many appeals, as parties will think they have been unfairly treated.
- (Michael Zander) Lord Woolf commissioned no research on what causes delay but blamed it on lawyers, yet other bodies, such as the Cantley Committee, suggested that the way lawyers operate the adversarial system is a minor cause of delay. "There is not the slightest prospect that these prescribed time limits will be complied with".
- (Zander) the RAND corporation has reached discourging conclusions in research on the effects of judicial case management in the U.S.A. in 1990–1995. It indicates that judges have difficulty in allocating cases to the right track at an early stage. Judges will vary in aptitude. Increasing their discretion will produce inconsistent decisions. Many new procedures will worsen delay. Case management will generate more work for lawyers and increase cost.
- (Adrian Zuckerman) The fixed costs of £2,500 for fast track cases is too much, once V.A.T., expert fees, interlocutory applications and advocacy fees have been added.
- (Zuckerman) "The cause of excessive cost lies not in the complexity of our procedure, but in the incentives that lawyers have to complicate litigation." These interests will defeat Woolf's attempts to reform. Lawyers paid by the hour have an incentive to complicate cases. Lay clients have no means of judging whether their solicitor's work is necessary (*e.g.* interlocutory applications). (Quoting Lord Mackay's White Paper

on legal aid reform) the legal aid system gives highest rewards to lawyers who do more work than is necessary.

- (J.A. Jolowicz) The reforms will effect a significant shift away from the adversary system. There is no reason why this should not be done, as adversarial civil justice grew out of jury trial, which is now almost extinct. If the Woolf proposals result in a move towards achieving the aim of substantive, as well as procedural justice, they are to be welcomed.
- Responses to the many objections to the Woolf report are made by District Judge Greenslade at [1997] N.L.J. 1147, 1215, 1252, 1293.

Implementation of Woolf

Many of the recommendations made in Lord Woolf's 1995 interim report had been implemented by 1996 and are listed in his final report. In May 1997, the Conservative Lord Chancellor was replaced by Labour's Lord Irvine. He appointed Peter Middleton to review both the Woolf Report and the reform of legal aid. In October 1997, Lord Irvine responded to Peter Middleton's report, in a speech to the Law Society, setting out the Labour Government's proposals for action in response to the Woolf report:

- Expand small claims jurisdiction to £5,000.
- Leave the small claims limit at £1,000 in personal injury cases.
- Accept Woolf's plans for judicial case management.
- Multi-track and fast track will be implemented by April, 1999 but fast track limit should be £15,000, not £10,000 as Woolf had suggested.
- Costs in the fast track will be fixed. Research on this is being conducted in 1997–1998.
- The cost of civil courts should be met by people who use them but the civil fee structure is "irrational and hopelessly out of date" so needs reforming. Exemptions from court fees should be extended to more groups on state benefits.

PRE-TRIAL CRIMINAL PROCEDURE

In 1990–1991, public faith in the English criminal justice system reached an all time low, with the official acknowledgment of a number of miscarriages of justice which had resulted in many innocent people wasting decades in gaol, only to be freed after years of campaigning by pressure groups and journalists had raised the cases to *causes célèbres* status. The most notable of these cases are those of *The Guildford Four, The Maguires, The Birmingham Six, The Winchester Three* and *The Broadwater Farm Three.*

In 1991, in response to public anxiety over all this, the Home Secretary appointed a Royal Commission on Criminal Justice, which reported in 1993. Its terms of reference were to examine the effectiveness of the Criminal Justice System in securing the conviction of the guilty and the acquittal of the innocent and to examine in particular:

1. the supervision by senior officers of police investigations;
2. the role of the prosecutor in supervising the gathering of evidence and arrangements for its disclosure to the defence;
3. the role of experts and the forensic science services;
4. access to experts and legal services by the defence;
5. the accused's opportunities to state his case;
6. the powers of the courts in direct proceedings, including the possibility of their having an investigative role during and pre-trial; uncorroborated confession evidence;
7. the role of the Court of Appeal;
8. arrangements for investigating miscarriages of justice when appeal rights have been exhausted.

In this section and the sections on trial and criminal appeals, I incorporate the main recommendations of the R.C.C.J.

There is only space here to mention the few most significant recommendations of the R.C.C.J. The Summary of Recommendations is reproduced at [1993] N.L.J. 993 and 1028. These recommendations have been heavily criticised, notably by lawyers, who have drawn attention to the number of recommendations which would ease the task of the prosecution, rather than strengthen protection for the defendant. This surprised commentators, in view of the fact that the Commission was set up in response to some of this century's most famous wrongful convictions. Students will find many critiques of the Commission's report in 1993 legal news journals (*e.g. New Law Journal* and *Legal Action* and, in more depth, in The *Criminal Law Review* for November and December 1993 and a special 1994 issue of the *Journal of Law and Society* entitled *Justice and Efficiency*).

Prosecution

The Prosecutors.

The Attorney-General. His consent is required by statute for prosecutions of national interest or sensitivity (*e.g.* certain prosecutions under the Official Secrets Act). He can also enter a *nolle prosequi*, to stop a prosecution (*e.g.* if it is vexatious or he discovers the defendant is dying).

The Director of Public Prosecutions. In addition to heading the Crown Prosecution Service, about 60 statutes require her consent to prosecution, mostly to serious offences, but she is very seldom involved personally in a decision. In 1997, the Law Commission suggested drastic reduction in the number of offences where the A.G.'s or D.P.P.'s consent is required.

Public bodies, with statutory prosecution powers (*e.g.* The Post Office, for T.V. licence offences, H.M. Customs and Excise for V.A.T. offences).

Private persons. Private prosecutions were preserved on the recommendation of the Royal Commission on Criminal Procedure (1980).

The Crown Prosecution Service. This was created as a national prosecution service by the Prosecution of Offences Act 1985, on the recommendation of the Royal Commission on Criminal Procedure. Until then, most prosecutions were instituted by the police, from individual constabularies. Critics, including *Justice*, thought this was anomalous, as most other legal systems used national prosecution services, and undesirable, as the decision to prosecute was not made independently.

The C.P.S. has the discretion to prosecute and stop proceedings. It can ask the police to investigate offences but it cannot order them to do so. It has no investigatory facilities. The R.C.C.J. considered whether the C.P.S. should have the power to supervise police investigations, as in Scotland or European jurisdictions. They decided against it but recommended strengthening police consultation with the C.P.S. in directing and furthering their investigations. They considered the high rates of discontinuance of prosecutions and directed acquittals and recommended that the C.P.S. be more vigilant in ensuring full preparation of cases coming to the Crown Court.

The C.P.S. are guided in their decisions whether to prosecute by their *Code For Crown Prosecutors* (1994). They apply a two stage evidential and public interest test.

The Evidential Test. The prosecutor must be satisfied that there is a realistic prospect of conviction: are a jury or magistrates more likely than not to convict? Is the evidence admissible and reliable? Are the witnesses strong enough?

The Public Interest Test. Prosecutors must balance factors for and against prosecution. Factors *for* include:

significant sentence likely, if convicted; weapon or violence used; offence premeditated; vulnerable victim; motivated by discrimination; offence widespread in the area.

Factors *against* include:

possible small penalty; minor harm or defendant has put it right; offence committed by mistake; long delay after offence; defendant infirm or young.

Bail

The Bail Act 1976 introduced a statutory right to bail. Magistrates may refuse bail only if they believe the defendant will fail to surrender to custody; or commit an offence or will interfere with witnesses. The court must have regard to the nature and seriousness of the offence and the probable disposal of the defendant, his character and community ties, etc., his previous bail record and the strength of evidence against him.

During the late 1980s concern arose over the number of offences committed whilst on bail. The Criminal Justice and Public Order Act 1994 adds another exception to the right to bail where the defendant was already on bail at the time of the alleged new offence. Further, it prohibits bail for those charged with murder, rape, manslaughter and attempts where they have previously been convicted of such an offence.

The Bail (Amendment) Act 1993 gives the prosecution a right to appeal to the Crown Court against the grant of bail by magistrates, in relation to certain serious offences. The accused is not entitled to be present at the appeal, if represented, and the Magistrates' Association opposed the Act on this ground.

Mode of Trial—Crown Court or Magistrates' Court?

Indictable cases have to be tried in the Crown Court and summary offences in the magistrates' court but in the category of median seriousness, "triable either way," the magistrates may send a case up to the Crown Court, if they consider it too serious, or the defendant may elect to be dealt with by the Crown Court. The R.C.C.J. inferred, from 1990 research by Moxon and Hederman, that too many Crown Court cases could more appropriately be dealt with in the magistrates' court. This resulted from defendants opting for Crown Court jury trial, then pleading guilty and from magistrates sending up unimportant cases. The R.C.C.J., very controversially, recommended removing the defendant's overriding right to choose jury trial. They reiterated that, while research had shown that the acquittal rate seemed to be higher in the Crown Court, it also showed that, in matched cases, sentencing was harsher and many defendants later regretted their decision to opt for the Crown Court.

Then, in 1995 the Home Office published a consultation paper on *Mode of Trial*. It suggested three options for resolving the problem identified by the R.C.C.J.: classify more offences as summary only, remove the defendant's right to elect or require magistrates to ask defendants to indicate their plea before taking a decision on mode of trial. The Government opted for the last of these, which is now enacted in section 49 of the Criminal Procedure and Investigations Act 1996. The intention behind this section is that magistrates will then hear summarily all either way cases where the defendant indicates a guilty plea, unless, of course, the magistrates consider their sentencing powers too low, in which case they retain the option of committing the defendant to the Crown Court. The aim is to shift yet more criminal business down from the Crown Court into the cheaper magistrates' court. Even before the section was brought into force, however, in February 1997, the Conservative Home Secretary introduced a consultation paper, *Review of Delay in the Criminal Justice System*. This again suggested dispensing with the defendant's trial option and leaving it to the magistrates to decide which court should hear the case. Three months later, the Labour Government replaced the Conservatives and, at the time of writing, early 1998, they are still considering this suggestion.

Committal Proceedings

Almost all defendants in the Crown Court have been committed for trial by magistrates, whose job it is to certify that there is a prima facie case against him. Mostly this is a quasi-administrative paper exercise, whereby the magistrates simply accept the defence lawyer's assurance that she is satisfied from the prosecution papers that there is a sufficient case against the defendant. The R.C.C.J. decided that committals serve no usseful purpose and should be replaced by simple transfer proceedings. The Government purported to enact this in the Criminal Justice and Public Order Act 1994 but the section and the delegated legislation made thereunder was deemed unworkable before it could be implemented, in 1995 so it was repealed in the Criminal Procedure and Investigation Act 1996 and replaced by modified committal proceedings in sections 44 and 47 and Schedule 1. All committals will become paper committals, abolishing the old style committal, which was still used occasionally and which required the examination of witnesses. Defendants may be sent straight to the Crown Court, without committal proceedings where a bill of indictment is preferred.

Pre-trial Disclosure of Evidence

At common law and in statute, requirements for pre-trial disclosure had become more extensive and complex since the 1980s. From 1981, the Attorney General had required the prosecution to make available to the defence all unused material, with certain exceptions. The picture became more complex after several miscarriages of justice in the 1990s and the courts found it difficult to strike a balance between the defendant's interest in seeing all the material gathered in the investigation and the prosecution's interest in keeping sensitive material (such as the identity of an informant). At the same time, inroads were made into the defendant's right of silence by requiring him to provide information in certain cases. For instance, expert evidence had to be disclosed, since 1987 and those charged with serious fraud could be faced with a list of written questions from the serious fraud office. The R.C.C.J. recommended a statutory scheme of disclosure. They were particularly anxious to stop "ambush defences", where an unpredictable defence is raised at trial. This was effected by sections 34–39 of the C.J.P.O. Act 1994, which qualifies the defendant's right of silence (see below).

The Criminal Procedure and Investigations Act 1996, Part I, enacts a statutory scheme of disclosure, which is being brought into force at the time of writing, 1998.

Primary disclosure by the prosecutor is required by section 3. He must disclose to the defence any previously undisclosed material which he has inspected, in accordance with a code and which in his opinion might undermine the prosecution case, or give to the accused a written statement that there is no such material. This section has been fiercely criticised by defence lawyers because the prosecutor will determine what he must disclose. Section 4 requires the prosecutor to give to the accused the schedule of non-sensitive material received by the prosecutor in accordance with a code of practice provided for under the Act.

Disclosure by the accused, which has also been subject to force-ful criticism, as eroding the presumption of innocence, is intro-duced by section 5. It requires the accused to give a defence state-ment to the court and to the prosecutor, if the case it to be heard in the Crown Court and if the prosecutor has fulfilled primary dis-closure. It is a written statement, setting out in general terms the nature of the accused's defence, indicating the matters on which he takes issue with the prosecution and giving the particulars of any alibi. Under section 6, the defendant may make a voluntary defence statement, if he is to be tried summarily. Section 7 provides for secondary prosecution disclosure of any previously undisclosed material, after the defence statement. Section 8 allows the accused to apply for disclosure of material by the prosecutor, where he has reasonable cause to believe there is previously undisclosed material which might aid his defence. Section 9 places a continuing duty on the prosecutor.

The prosecutor need not disclose material which has been obtained by interception of communication (which means phone-tapping, etc.) or where the prosecutor concludes it is not in the public interest to do so (such as information from an informant). Section 11 allows the court to comment and to draw "such infer-ences as appear proper" where the defence disclosure is defective or too late. The Home Secretary is empowered to make regulations about the timing of disclosure.

Sections 14 and 15 allow the defendant to seek a court review of a non-disclosure decision. The court must rule whether non-disclosure is in the public interest. Whether disclosure is in the public interest will still be determined by the old common law rules. Otherwise, the statute replaces common law.

Plea Bargaining

This can mean one of two things:

1. A deal between prosecution and defence, as described above, where the prosecution drop a serious charge in

exchange for a guilty plea to a lesser charge (charge bargaining).

2. A change of plea from not guilty to guilty in exchange for a lower sentence.

This first is endemic and well-known in the Crown Court and equally widespread but less publicised in the magistrates' courts.

The second, well-known and widely used in the United States, is illegal and impracticable here because judges cannot take part in it (see *Turner*) and our prosecutors cannot recommend sentences.

The effects of plea bargaining and other pressures on the accused to plead guilty are the topic of much socio-legal research (notably Baldwin and McConville's *Negotiated Justice* (1977) and Bottoms & McClean's *Defendants in The Criminal Process* (1976)) but, sadly, we only have space to examine the legal position: *R. v. Turner* (CA 1970) affirmed by a 1976 Practice Direction, held that:

(a) Counsel can advise the defendant (how to plead) in strong terms provided he makes it clear the defendant has a free choice.

(b) There must be free access between counsel and judge but any discussion with the judge must take place before both counsel.

(c) Generally, the judge should "never indicate the sentence which he is minded to impose" and never indicate he would impose a severer sentence following a "not guilty" plea.

(d) He may not indicate that, having read the papers, he would impose a certain type of sentence, following a guilty plea.

(e) A judge *may* say that, whatever the plea, the sentence will take a particular form.

The R.C.C.J. recommended that the system of rewarding defendants for pleading guilty should be formalised. The earlier the guilty plea, the higher the sentence discount. Judges should be permitted to indicate, in advance of trial, the highest sentence they were prepared to give. The late Lord Chief Justice Taylor has spoken out against this recommendation and in favour of *Turner*. Only the first part of the recommendation has been enacted in section 48 of the Criminal Justice and Public Order Act 1994. This puts a duty on the court, in sentencing a guilty pleader, to take into account the stage at which he pleaded guilty and to announce in open court any resultant sentence reduction. This, of course, simply formalises the existing system of rewards for early guilty pleas. It does not introduce plea bargaining as the Americans know it but it may affect (c), above.

The Plea and Directions Hearing

A 1995 Practice Direction requires these hearings prior to Crown Court trials. They are very brief, designed to prepare for the trial and fix a trial date. In all class one or serious or complex cases, the prosecution provides a summary, identifying issues of law and fact and estimating trial length. The accused is arraigned and his plea entered. Following a not guilty plea, the parties are expected to inform the court of witnesses and any special requirements for trial. If the plea is guilty, the judge should, if possible, proceed to sentence, after hearing a plea in mitigation. Where the judge is considering a custodial sentence or non-custodial alternative, she may require a pre-sentence report or, where appropriate, a psychiatric or medical report.

Pre-trial Hearings

These are not new but have been put onto a statutory footing by Parts III and IV of the Criminal Procedure and Investigations Act 1996. Prior to the swearing in of the jury, the judge may order a preparatory hearing for one of the following purposes: identifying important issues; assisting the jury's comprehension of those issues; expediting proceedings or assisting the judge's trial management. She may hear arguments and rule on points of law and admissibility of evidence. She may require detailed case statements and require the prosecution evidence and any explanatory material to be prepared in a form which she considers is likely to help the jury understand it. Judges have always heard such arguments in the absence of the jury but dealing with these questions pre-trial may prevent interruptions of the trial, where the jury are sent out and kept waiting. They are modelled on preparatory hearings in serious or complex frauds, made under the Criminal Justice Act 1987.

THE TRIAL PROCESS GENERALLY

Here we examine the characteristics of the trial in the adversarial process. The trial is its focal point but it must be remembered that a trial occurs in only a tiny minority of cases. The vast majority of defendants in the criminal courts plead guilty and so appear only to offer a plea in mitigation and to be sentenced and, in the civil courts, most cases are settled or judgment is entered in default. If the percentage of cases contested increased slightly, the court system would collapse.

It is important to understand that there are significant differences between civil and criminal trials, such as the degree of proof required and evidential differences, such as the rule against hearsay. The adversarial model cannot apply as well to criminal trials as it does to civil because the defendant is faced with such a powerful opponent: the state.

The Concept of Judge as Arbiter

The essence of the role of the English judge, or magistrate, is that he acts as an unbiased umpire whose job it is to listen to evidence presented to him by both sides, without interfering in the trial process. This is often contrasted with the role of European first instance judges who perform an inquisitorial role, themselves directing criminal investigations, cross-examining the defendant and collecting evidence for the trial court. Of course, there is no comparable English equivalent.

The Practical Meaning of Judge as Arbiter

1. Summoning witnesses. The judge and court do not select witnesses. It is left to the parties to call the witnesses they see fit to boost their case. The civil judge (at least, at the time of writing, in 1998 but see Woolf above) has no power to call witnesses unless both parties consent. In criminal cases the judge does have such power but it is used very rarely. This can have two undesirable results.

(a) There may be conflict between expert witnesses, where each side has an opposing expert and the judge has no power to call an independent adviser for himself. It may be that such conflicts are reduced slightly in civil trials by the compulsory exchange of expert evidence, pre-trial, and by a rule operating since 1986, in cases other than those on personal injuries, whereby the court can direct a meeting between experts to see whether they can agree a report. Nevertheless, a judge (and jury) will still frequently find themselves having to decide between two experts in a criminal case (*e.g.* on psychiatric or forensic evidence). The R.C.C.J. recommended preparatory hearings of expert witnesses before criminal trials, to try to resolve pre-trial as much conflict as possible.

Lord Woolf, commissioned by Lord Chancellor Mackay to over-haul civil procedure, suggests that the civil trial judge, not the parties, should have the power to call an expert.

(b) It may lead to a vital witness not being called where he would give penetrating evidence against both sides or on behalf of the defence, in a criminal trial. The failure of defence lawyers to discover or call essential defence witnesses has resulted in many notorious miscarriages of justice. The R.C.C.J. urged judges in criminal trials to use their powers to call such a witness and to question counsel as to why a witness had not been called.

2. The conduct of the trial. The judge does not interfere in the presentation of evidence by examining and cross-examining witnesses him or herself. This is left to the parties or their advocates. The role of the judge was set down clearly by Lord Denning M.R. in *Jones v. National Coal Board* (CA 1957) and can be summarised thus: he should:

(a) listen to all the evidence, only interfering to clarify neglected or obscure points;
(b) see that advocates behave and stick to the rules;
(c) exclude irrelevancies and discourage repetition;
(d) make sure he understands the advocates' points;
(e) at the end, make up his mind where the truth lies.

3. The judge's expertise on law and fact. Generally speaking, the judge relies on the advocates to present legal and factual arguments. Of course, the specialist judges of, say, the Admiralty Court, are appointed because they need a certain level of understanding to appreciate specialist argument but they do not choose which precedents to examine. A judge can, if a vital precedent has been ignored, invite counsel's arguments upon it. In tribunals, of course, panel members are appointed because of their factual expertise, the antithesis of a county court or High Court general list judge, who is meant to be a Jack-of-all-trades.

The rule of non-intervention, set out above, does not apply to *legal* argument addressed to the judge. Students watching this in court will see that very often a dialogue goes on between counsel and the judge, especially in civil cases and the appellate courts. If Lord Woolf's recommendations are followed, civil judges may become much more interventionist in all aspects of case management.

English law is emphatic that the judge or magistrates or magistrates' clerk must not interfere in a case. To do so invokes accusation of a breach of natural justice. Justice must be seen to be done. Bias need not be proven for proceedings to be quashed: *R. v. Sussex Justices, ex p. McCarthy* (HC 1924).

The rule of non-interference is subject to certain exceptions:

(a) Small Claims in the county court. Research by Appleby (1978) showed some registrars employed an inquisitorial technique. Many of those who appear are unrepresented and, therefore, the progress of the case depends on the district judge being somewhat interventionist. The Civil Justice Review recommended that district judges adopt a more standardised inquisitorial role in small claims and the C.L.S.A., s.6 provides for the County Court Rules to prescribe the manner of taking and questioning evidence.

(b) The Unrepresented. The plight of the unrepresented has been well documented in socio-legal research (Dell (1971), Carlen (1976), Darbyshire (1984)). Where a defendant is unrepresented, mostly in the magistrates' courts, as virtually all Crown Court defendants are represented, he is wholly dependent on the goodwill and expertise of the Bench or, more realistically, the clerk, to help him put his case and examine witnesses and explain what is being asked of him, *e.g.* choice of venue in a triable-either-way offence. Some clerks are much more prepared and skilled to help than others.

(c) Matrimonial Proceedings. Under the Magistrates' Courts Act 1980 the court is under a duty to help the unrepresented party, in family proceedings, to present their evidence.

The Role of the Magistrates' Clerk

When examining the role of the judge in the adversarial system, it is essential to remember to examine the peculiar role of the magistrates' clerk.

The legal position of the clerk is set down in an amalgam of case law, statute and Practice Directions. Amazingly, a magistrates' court is correctly constituted without a clerk, even though lay magistrates are wholly dependent on their clerks for advice on law, practice, procedure and sentencing. The court clerk, by far the most prevalent legal adviser to magistrates, enjoyed no legal recognition whatever in this role until the enactment of section 117 of the C.L.S.A. 1990. The justices' clerk's advisory role is set out in the Justices of the Peace Act 1997, s.45. It "declares" his functions to include giving advice to justices, on request, about law, practice and procedure and empowers him to draw the magistrates' attention to these matters at any time.

The courts are prepared to allow a great deal of latitude to the clerk to regulate the progress of a case and the proceedings before her. A 1981 Practice Direction clarified the position by encouraging the clerk to offer advice in open court in those cases where the magistrates had not requested it but in *R. v. Uxbridge Magistrates' Court, ex p. Smith* (1985), the High Court held it was not necessary for the clerk's advice on law to be given in open court.

The Adversarial Method of Eliciting Witnesses' Evidence

Eliciting evidence by the question and answer method. The parties are kept to a fixed order of speeches:

(a) Prosecution or plaintiff makes his opening speech.
(b) His first witness is examined by him or his legal representative.
(c) This witness is then cross-examined by the opposition.
(d) Each witness is so examined until the end of the prosecution/plaintiff's case.
(e) Traditionally, this allowed the defendant to see the whole of the case against him, before exposing his defence which put him at an advantage. This is now massively qualified by pre-trial disclosure required by defendants tried on indictment and, in civil cases by the exchange of skeleton arguments and document bundles.
(f) The defendant is examined by the defence advocate then cross-examined by the prosecution/plaintiff.
(g) All the defence witnesses are so questioned.
(h) The defence sum up.
(i) The plaintiff/prosecution may reply.

This is meant to guarantee "fair play." In criminal trials each witness stays outside until called, so as not to copy and is kept strictly to answering the questions put. If he tries to add points he feels relevant, or pass an opinion, he is quickly stopped by the judge or advocates. This results in two things:

(i) If the witness feels he has vital evidence to add, he has no way of volunteering it. This can be especially frustrating to expert witnesses, examined by non-experts. The R.C.C.J. recommended that where expert evidence is disputed in criminal trials, the judge should invite the expert witness to say whether they wish to add to their evidence.

(ii) This system is very heavily dependent on the expertise of the advocate, to bring out all and only that relevant information helpful to his case.

The rule against leading questions. Counsel are not allowed to "lead" their own witnesses, *i.e.* ask questions which suggest an answer, unless the judge and opposition consent. The very aim of cross-examination is, however, to mislead.

The R.C.C.J. recommended that, in criminal trials, the judge should act firmly to control bullying or intimidatory tactics by counsel. Also, if questioning is protracted as a time wasting tactic, the judge should be empowered to reduce counsel's fees.

THE CRIMINAL TRIAL

To call our trial accusatorial and the continental civil law system inquisitorial is a crude over simplification. It leads to people extolling the virtues of English law by claiming that, in England, one is innocent until proven guilty whereas "over there" it is the other way round. The presumption of innocence "dear to the hearts of Englishmen," says Glanville Williams in *The Proof of Guilt* (1963), really means just that the burden of proof is on the prosecution. You are neither presumed innocent nor guilty.

Nevertheless, the defendant is provided with certain safeguards in the criminal trial, to tip the balance slightly against the heavy weight of the State. Consider them as did the R.C.C.J. and evaluate whether they are fair enough or over generous. Critics of the R.C.C.J. say that most of its recommendations and consequent legislation tilt the balance back towards enhancing the power of the prosecution, especially the modification of the right to silence (see below) and the requirement for pre-trial disclosure (see above).

The Quantum of Proof

The criminal quantum of proof is proof "beyond reasonable doubt." This means that it should be more difficult for the prosecutor to satisfy the jury or magistrates of the guilt of the defendant than it is for the plaintiff to satisfy the civil trial judge of a civil defendant's liability. The civil quantum of proof is "on the balance of probabilities." An ideal quantum of proof would convict all the guilty and acquit all the innocent but this is Utopian. Some error is inherent, and English law prefers (at least, in theory) to err on the side of acquitting a few guilty ones, as epitomised by Blackstone: "It is better that ten guilty men go free than one innocent man should suffer." Thus, these rules are meant to protect the defendant: the quantum of proof, the fact that he sees the prosecution case exposed first (now subject to pre-trial review in certain magistrates' courts and the C.J.P.O. Act 1994), and certain exclusory rules of evidence:

The Exclusory Rules of Evidence

Certain evidence is excluded because it is unduly prejudicial against the defendant, inherently unreliable, or its utterance is against the public interest:

(a) Defendant's previous convictions. BUT the exceptions to this are important. His record *is* admissible if:

(i) the defendant puts his character in issue (*i.e.* starts claiming to possess an unsullied past);

(ii) he attacks prosecution witnesses (*e.g.* says the police kicked him down the steps to the cells);

(iii) he has previously been *charged with* a similar offence in similar circumstances; or

(iv) he attacks a co-accused.

The R.C.C.J. recommended that (iii) above should be extended. Where the defendant admits the basic facts alleged by the prosecution and the question is only one of knowledge or intent, the fact that he or she has *previous similar convictions* should be made known to the jury so the admission of previous convictions should not be limited to cases where there is a "striking similarity" in the evidence. The Law Commission produced a paper on the admission of previous misconduct, in 1996 but it produced diverse reactions.

(b) Spouses. Spouses are competent but not compellable for the defence but not normally competent for the prosecution.

(c) Communications between client and legal adviser, without permission.

(d) Identification evidence. Not surprising in the light of psychological findings on human memory, this is a very unreliable type of evidence and, as the cases published by *Justice* amply demonstrate, the source of many wrongful convictions. It has been the subject of repeated scrutiny (*e.g.* by the *11th Report of the Criminal Law Revision Committee* (1972) and the *Devlin Committee Report* (1976)). This led to a ruling by the Court of Appeal (*R. v. Turner* (1977)) that the judge should warn the jury of the dangers of relying on it.

(e) Hearsay evidence. The basic rule against hearsay (which applied to both civil and criminal proceedings) is quite simply this: evidence may not be related to the court unless its author is there to present it. It applies to both the related spoken word and to documents. It is thought to be inherently unfair to rely on the evidence of a witness who is not present to be cross-examined. Unfortunately, the hearsay rule is subject to so many exceptions that it is very difficult of application, in practice. Here are some of the exceptions:

(i) Statements of the dead, the unfit, the untraceable, etc., business documents and expert evidence, all provided for in the Criminal Justice Act 1988, ss.23–30.
(ii) Admissions or confessions.
(iii) *Res gestae*, or statements spontaneous and contemporaneous with the event (*e.g.* accusation by a victim of an attack, within minutes).
(iv) Written witness statements.

The hearsay rule has been eroded even further in relation to civil evidence and the Civil Justice Review invited the Lord Chancellor to commission an inquiry into its usefulness. It was eventually abolished by the Civil Evidence Act 1995, following a report by the Law Commission. The R.C.C.J. recommended that hearsay be admitted to a greater degree than at present, in criminal trials, but that the rule should be examined by the Law Commission. They reported in 1995.

(f) Confessions obtained by oppression or in consequence of anything said or done which, in the circumstances, rendered the confession unreliable. The burden of proving that a confession was not so obtained is on the prosecution (Police and Criminal Evidence Act 1984, s.76). The R.C.C.J. recommended strengthening safeguards for the accused against the admission of unreliable confessions. The trial judge should be empowered to stop any case if the prosecution case is demonstrably unsafe or too weak to go to the jury. Any taped confession, unconfirmed by the accused, should be inadmissible. They recommended that the jury should be warned of the great dangers of convicting on confession evidence alone, where there is no supporting evidence. Disappointing many critics, however, the R.C.C.J. did not recommend a requirement that confession evidence be corroborated.

(g) Unfairly obtained evidence (PACE 1984, s.78).

The Right to Silence

Until The Criminal Justice And Public Order Act 1994, the defendant had an unfettered right to silence, both in the police station and in court. In court, this extended to the right not to be asked questions and the judge could comment on it but not adversely. The right was considered by the Criminal Law Revision Committee (1972), the Royal Commission on Criminal Procedure (1981) and the R.C.C.J. and it has long been a subject of controversy. The arguments about the rule go thus:

Proponents. hail it as a major (almost symbolic) safeguard of the English legal system that the defendant cannot convict himself out of his own mouth. It leaves the burden of proof entirely on the prosecution.

Opponents. say (i) it is a rule protecting the guilty (ii) it encourages the police to intimidate suspects into confessing (iii) it is sentimental to argue that the accused should not be allowed to convict himself.

Limitations Proposed. Since 1987 Conservative Home Secretaries had been considering limiting the accused's right not to have adverse inferences made, in court, of his exercise of the right of silence in the police station and in 1988 they promised legislation to limit the right in certain circumstances. Lawyers claim this was the result of police pressure. A Home Office working party examined the right of silence but was disbanded.

Prior to 1994, one major inroad into the right, which has wrought some criticism, was the power of the Serious Fraud Office to demand answers to certain questions, when gathering evidence. The Office has used this power frequently. In *Saunders v. United Kingdom* (E.C.H.R. 1996) the European Court of Human Rights ruled that powers exercised by the D.T.I., under the Companies Act 1985, to require a defendant to answer questions put to him pre-trial, offended against the Convention on Human Rights.

The R.C.C.J. considered the right of silence pre-trial and at trial. They recommended that the former should be retained and that only after the prosecution case had been fully disclosed should the defendant be required to answer the charges made, at the risk of adverse comment at trial on any new, undisclosed defence (an "ambush defence").

The Criminal Justice and Public Order Act 1994 goes much further than this and, critics would say, effectively abrogates both stages of the right to silence. Sections 34–39 allow the court to draw "such inferences as appear proper" from the accused's failure to mention, under police questioning, any fact which he could have been expected to mention, or failure (under questioning) to account for any objects, marks or substances, or failure (under questioning) to account for his presence at a particular place, or failure to give evidence or answer questions at trial.

5. ACCESS TO JUSTICE

If the Rule of Law states that everyone should be equal before the law then I would argue that this implies that everyone should have equal access to the law and to justice. This means, broadly: being able to make full use of legal rights, through adequate legal services, *i.e.* advice, assistance and representation, regardless of means; also, the ability to make full use of the court structure and rights of appeal.

Those issues are dealt with in this chapter and above, in relation to the adversarial process (*e.g.* Civil Justice Review).

LEGAL AID

This phrase has two meanings. *Generically*: state funded legal representation, advice and assistance, carried out by a barrister or solicitor. *More specifically*: representation and ancillary work (*e.g.* preparation). *Legal advice and assistance* falls under "legal aid" but refers to all help falling short of representation: advice, letter writing, telephone calls, etc. and assistance by way of representation (ABWOR).

Here, I describe the legal aid system in the context of a critical analysis of the Legal Aid Act 1988 and developments since 1988. This states the law at the time of writing BUT the reader should note that the Labour Government is currently (1998) considering whether to restructure the funding and delivery of legal services. They may set up a new framework and repeal, or significantly amend the Legal Aid Act 1988 (see below).

The Legal Aid Act 1988

The *purpose* of the statute is outlined in section 1, to establish a new "framework" for publicly funded advice, assistance and representation "with a view to helping persons who might otherwise be unable to obtain (it) on account of their means."

The Legal Aid Board (section 3) administers legal aid, replacing the function of the Law Society, as the Government's *Efficiency Scrutiny Report* (1986) thought it undesirable that the profession, remunerated by legal aid funds, should hold the purse-strings.

The Board's powers (section 4). The Board may consider and advise the Lord Chancellor on legal services policy. To this end, it both responds to his requests for advice and initiates its own investigations.

Its franchising proposals have proved highly controversial. The Board was given wide powers to *"contract out"* the provision of certain legal services to "persons or bodies" (other than lawyers in private practice).

Aware of hostility from solicitors, the Board adopted the notion of "franchising" as less provocative than this alternative. They have offered fixed term, renewable contracts to firms of solicitors as franchisees to deliver legal services under certain categories, *e.g.* family, housing, employment, welfare, immigration, personal injury. Franchisees are empowered to determine all green form and ABWOR applications and extensions and even emergency Legal Aid certificates but must satisfy certain requirements, such as independence, non-discrimination, expertise in welfare benefits, an adequate library and efficiency in case management and in keeping clients informed. The Law Society originally threatened a boycott so the Legal Aid Board spent 1993–1994 trying to persuade the Law Society to endorse the franchising scheme and to encourage more offices to apply for franchises, by amending the contract requirements and by assuring solicitors that it does not aim to develop a system of competitive tendering. The first franchises were granted in August 1994. From 1995, the Legal Aid Board piloted the first non-solicitor franchises, granted to advisers unsupervised by solicitors (*e.g.* CAB workers) and, since 1996, more of such non-solicitor agencies have been franchised. In 1997, the Board began experimenting with three different· models of block contract funding for civil non-family advice, involving 120 firms. They established separate pilots for criminal duty solicitor work and family mediation services (provided under the Family Law Act 1996).

The Board has power to *make grants and loans*, which has enabled it to take over the funding of several law centres, although the Law Society failed to amend the Bill to provide for specific funding for them.

The Board's duties (section 5). They must *report annually* to the Lord Chancellor. The Law Society proposed a (failed) amendment that this should contain statistics of the percentage of households currently eligible for legal aid. This reflects an anxiety that the Government, in economising, is reducing this percentage. From 1992, the Conservative Lord Chancellor made drastic reductions in eligibility. Non-contributory aid became unavailable to all those living on incomes above the level of income support, including those on state retirement pensions or invalidity benefit.

Advice and assistance (Part III). This Part gives the Lord Chancellor wide powers but, for the time being, he has preserved the *green form scheme*, under which advice and assistance, up to a certain limit (two hours' worth, or three hours' worth in matrimonial cases) is mostly given by solicitors in private practice, after they have conducted a means test on the client. Contributions are payable above a certain level of disposable income and capital, according to a sliding scale, which makes allowance for dependants. The means tests for civil and criminal legal aid (described below) follow the same pattern but with different monetary limits. As these are updated annually, they are not published here.

The Lord Chancellor may provide for free green form advice. This power is currently used to provide advice under the duty solicitor scheme, for example. He may also exclude certain topics from the green form scheme and he has used this power to exclude wills and conveyancing, with certain exceptions, from green form advice.

The Act preserves the notorious *statutory charge* on advice and assistance (section 11) and civil legal aid (section 16), under which the cost of legal aid can be recovered from an assisted person, over and above her contribution, from any property or costs recovered. This may destroy the benefit of her litigation and critics have long sought its abolition.

The Act also preserves another heavily criticised power, which can *penalise unassisted parties* who litigate successfully against a legally aided opponent. Costs may only be awarded against the legally aided party if she instituted proceedings *and* the court is satisfied the unassisted party would otherwise suffer severe financial hardship *and* if it is just and equitable that they should recover costs from public funds (sections 13 and 18). Lord Denning M.R. called this rule "the ugly, unacceptable face of British justice," in *Thew v. Reeves* (CA 1981).

ABWOR (assistance by way of representation) appeared in the Legal Aid Act 1979. The Lord Chancellor introduced it for domestic cases, in magistrates' courts and extended it, in 1982, to mental health review tribunals. In 1997, it was extended to persons at risk of imprisonment for failing to obey a court order and prisoners detained at Her Majesty's pleasure, following a ruling of the ECHR that failure to provide aid to a community charge defaulter was a breach of Articles 6(1) and 3(c) of the European Convention on Human Rights.

Civil legal aid (Part IV). The Lord Chancellor has power (section 14) to extend or restrict the categories of court or tribunal for which legal aid is available and Schedule 2 lists them and lists exclusions: for example, defamation proceedings.

Legal aid is currently provided for *only three tribunal systems*, The Employment Appeal Tribunal, Lands Tribunal and Commons Commissioners. Critics have long argued that legal aid should be available before all tribunals and research suggests that representation enhances the litigant's chances of success (*e.g.* Genn and Genn, 1989). The policy behind exclusion was, originally, an attempt to keep tribunals informal, by discouraging lawyers. Lawyers nevertheless do appear, for those who can afford them, and some tribunals have become very legalistic.

Another gap in the provision of civil legal aid is that it is not automatically available for *appeals to the House of Lords*, as it is in criminal appeals (where the prosecutor appeals—section 21). Arguably, the state should pay for House of Lords appeals as their opinions are as crucial in developing the law as the work of Parliament.

Under section 14, the Lord Chancellor can extend provision of legal aid, in terms of the applicant's capacity. The Law Society has urged that this power be used to permit *legal aid for class actions* or groups. There is still concern over how to fund group actions, *e.g.* on medical negligence and disasters, and the Legal Aid Board has produced two consultation papers on "multi-party actions" (the second in 1994).

The Lord Chancellor retains power to stipulate means and merits tests (section 15). On *merits*, statute requires that the applicant satisfies the Board that he has reasonable grounds for taking or defending proceedings not more appropriately dealt with by ABWOR. In practice, the granting committees scrutinise the "cost efficiency" of the action and decide whether they would advise an unassisted client to risk his own money.

On the *means test*, the upper income limit, above which a person is disentitled to legal aid, is now so low that only the very poor and the very rich can afford to use, say, the High Court.

The Act introduced a heavily criticised power to recoup *contributions* throughout the period of representation (section 16). Critics said this would encourage the assisted party's opponent to prolong litigation, to induce a settlement.

Criminal legal aid. This is subject to a different *means* test. Contributions, on a sliding scale, are mandatory. *Justices' clerks* can grant legal aid. In practice, this means a court clerk.

The availability of criminal legal aid in the Crown Court causes little concern, since about 97 per cent of defendants there are aided. Problems arise in magistrates' courts where diverse policies are exercised by clerks and their benches leading to a massively different rate of grant from court to court.

The reason for these discrepancies is that the *merits test* for criminal legal aid, retained by section 21, is open to subjectively different interpretation: "Representation may be granted where it appears ... desirable to do so in the interests of justice." This test has been applied in accordance with "the Widgery criteria," guidelines devised in 1966. These criteria, despite criticism (*e.g.* by the Royal Commission on Legal Services, 1979), are incorporated, in slightly modified form, in statute (section 22), requiring the court to take account of the following factors:

(a) likelihood of a sentence depriving the accused of liberty, livelihood; or serious damage to reputation;

(b) substantial question of law;

(c) inability of understanding;

(d) the nature of the defence involves tracing and interviewing witnesses or expert cross-examination;

(e) a third party interest in the accused's being represented.

Socio-legal research by Young, Moloney and Sanders (1992) demonstrates how differently court clerks interpret these criteria. Further guidance has been issued, in 1994, to attempt to secure consistency and regulations passed to require the recording of reasons for grant or refusal. In 1997, the House of Commons Public Accounts Committee heavily criticised magistrates' clerks' administration of the means test and their lack of accountability The Lord Chancellor's Department explained this was one reason why responsibility for criminal legal aid will be transferred to the Legal Aid Board in 2000–2001.

Lawyers' remuneration. The Lord Chancellor retains the power to fix fees by regulation (section 34).

The Act abandoned the principle of "fair and reasonable remuneration" for work done, in favour of standard fees. The Lord Chancellor, in 1992, used this power to fix fees for magistrates' court cases, with standard rates for guilty pleas and not guilty pleas etc. Lawyers launched a vigorous opposition campaign, arguing that there would be no incentive to spend extra hours preparing and researching a thorough defence case, thus no opportunity to root out a miscarriage of justice. In July 1997, the newly appointed Lord Chancellor Irvine blamed some of the excessive cost of criminal legal aid on "fat cat Q.C.s", whose fees are not fixed.

The Rising Cost of Legal Aid: Another Lord Chancellor's Review

In the autumn of 1990, the Conservative Lord Chancellor made several speeches signalling his concern over the rising cost of legal aid. He pointed to the gross cost of legal aid, £715 million, which had doubled in five years, and warned that the legal aid fund was not to be regarded as a "blank cheque." Since then, the cost of legal aid seems to be growing out of control. For instance, the net cost to the taxpayer in 1993–1994 was £1.021 million, an increase of 11.4 per cent over the previous year. The number of acts of assistance has increased in the 1990s, despite the massive cuts in eligibility. Some reasons for this are the expansion of assistance under the Children Act 1989 and an increase in advice at police stations. The cost of the average case has consistently risen above the rate of inflation.

In the meantime, Lord Chancellor Mackay established a three year review of eligibility for civil legal aid, which published a consultation paper in June 1991. It set out five major alternatives to the current system: The litigant's own resources, bank loans, contingency fees (the subject of another consultation paper), compulsory legal expenses insurance, and the option most discussed by Lord Mackay: the "safety net." Under this last alternative, the litigant pays for the cost of his/her case up to £2,000–3,000, before legal aid takes over. The obvious problem here is the unpredictable costs of the other side, should the litigant prove unsuccessful and the fact that the system is likely to put off impecunious litigants, even with meritorious cases.

In his speeches, Lord Chancellor Mackay demonstrated that he was also keen to question the very need for litigation and traditional forms of dispute resolution. He was keen to promote A.D.R., for instance. The Conservatives produced a Green Paper then a 1996 White Paper, *Striking the Balance*, setting out plans for controlling the cost of legal services but the Conservative Government was replaced in 1997 by Labour who are, at the time of writing, conducting their own review of legal aid funding. Lord Chancellor Irvine has announced, however, that he shares his predecessor's concern that spending must be curbed.

ALTERNATIVE LEGAL SERVICES

The traditional pattern for the provision of legal services, through the medium of the solicitor and/or barrister in private practice, paid for by the client, or by the statutory legal aid scheme, is only part of the picture. Because of gaps left by the traditional pattern, "unmet legal need" is generated and alternative services have been developed to try and meet it.

Unmet Need For Legal Services

This means individuals or groups have problems which are amenable to a legal solution but which do not receive one. The Marre Report identified the biggest area of unmet need as for advice on social welfare law, including housing, immigration and debt.

Causes:

1. The creation of new categories of legal rights, without the funding to enforce them (The Marre Report).
2. People may not realise they have a legal problem, for instance, they may be in dispute with a landlord or local authority and not know that a lawyer could help. Sometimes, professional advisers, such as social workers, may not recommend legal help because they too have failed to identify the problem as legal or because of traditional antipathy between the two professions.
3. Poverty: fear of high lawyers' fees; ignorance of the legal aid scheme.
4. Fear of authority: suspicion and fear of the Establishment, including lawyers; intimidation by legal jargon.
5. Inaccessibility of lawyers: solicitors open up offices in commercial centres of towns, rather than the outskirts or the country and they predominate in rich areas, *e.g.* the R.C.L.S. found one solicitor's office per 2,000 people in Bournemouth but only one per 66,000 in Huyton.
6. Lawyers' training has traditionally concentrated on lucrative business, *e.g.* revenue, company, commercial, conveyancing, property, not welfare law.

Law Centres

These are staffed by salaried solicitors, articled clerks and non-legally qualified experts, sometimes called "para-legals." They are financed by local or central government or charity, or the Legal Aid Board, and receipts from legally aided work, or a mixture (see below). They are established in poor areas (now about 52 in England and Wales, including the first mobile advice centre, launched in Carlisle, in 1996.) They develop a "shop front" image to attract clients and combat fear of lawyers. They are run by management committees and represented by the Law Centres Federation which provides a co-ordinating and political function and training.

History. The first law centres were established in the 1970s, amidst great opposition from the Law Society. They established a barrier to solicitors practising in law centres. To gain a practising certificate, they need a "waiver" of professional restrictive rules. To this, the Society attaches a condition forbidding them from working on a list of legal topics, usually comprising: conveyancing, company, commercial, probate, divorce, personal injury and adult crime.

Since 1970, the Society has reversed its stance on law centres and now fully supports them. It has learned through experience that local firms benefit from the existence of a law centre in the vicinity by referrals of clients it cannot or will not deal with.

Work. Apart from individual casework, such as tribunal representation, some centres prefer working for groups, not individuals, since an individual problem may be symptomatic of a more widespread one, *e.g.* local authority tenants against their landlord, women's groups and ethnic minority groups.

As well as providing legal services, law centres see their role as educative and campaigning (*e.g.* against individual targets and for law reform). They visit schools and community groups to educate on legal rights.

Problems. Apart from a high turnover of staff and generally a larger clientele than they can deal with, law centres have always suffered vulnerable funding. Both central and local government funding is subject to political change and several law centres have closed when funds have dried up, sometimes re-opening. Often, they run on short term grants from central or local government and/or charity plus legal aid earnings and there are always some who do not know where their next year's budget is coming from. All this is exacerbated by the fact that the law centre may find itself campaigning against the hand that feeds it, *i.e.* central or local government.

The R.C.L.S. recommended a nationwide network of centres, funded by government and administered by a quango but the Government stated, in 1985, that they viewed demands and funding for law centres as a local matter and this has recently been reiterated. The Lord Chancellor permitted the Legal Aid Board to take over grant aid to several law centres receiving government funds but has made it clear that this must not be extended.

Legal Advice Centres of which the Legal Aid Efficiency Scrutiny (1986) identified about 600, are sometimes attached to Citizen's Advice Bureaux, or universities. Lawyers give free advice, often in the evenings. If the client needs more, he may be referred to a solicitor.

Citizen's Advice Bureaux were much favoured by the R.C.L.S. They found that half their client problems had a legal content and their workers are well trained in identifying legal problems. Some Bureau workers represent people in tribunals and small claims.

Trade Unions. The R.C.L.S. found about half responding unions had legal departments to advise members.

Community groups, campaigning interest groups and advice centres, *e.g.* housing advice centres, MIND, the Child Poverty Action Group, the Automobile Association, all provide legal advice and sometimes fund legal representation for their members/clients.

OTHER IMPROVEMENTS IN ACCESS TO JUSTICE

Duty solicitor schemes. By 1982, there were schemes in 130 magistrates' courts, organised by local solicitors. Following R.C.L.S. recommendations, the Legal Aid Act 1982 provided for a national scheme.

The Police and Criminal Evidence Act 1984 provided for a national scheme in police stations, activated in late 1986. Under both, advice is given free and funding, supervision and policy development are provided by the Legal Aid Board.

Following a heavily critical research report, in 1990, by Bridges and Sanders, which disclosed a reluctance on the part of duty solicitors to attend police stations, the Board tightened up the scheme's obligations on solicitors. Generally speaking, they must now offer initial telephone advice and attend in specified circumstances. Given the poor rates of legal aid remuneration and the unsocial hours involved, some solicitors say it is not surprising that some duty solicitor schemes have already collapsed and the Board has failed to attract satisfactory replacements by contracting out.

Conditional fees were provided for under the C.L.S.A., and permitted from 1995. In certain actions, *e.g.* personal injury, actions before the ECHR, a plaintiff may agree with a solicitor to make an uplift in the fee in the event that the action is successful. Distinguish from American style *contingency fees*, where lawyer agrees with client to act on a no-win, no-fee basis and takes a percentage of damages recovered. In October 1997, Lord Irvine suggested replacing legal aid for damages claims with a conditional fee scheme (see below).

Pro Bono. In the 1990s Liberty persuaded big firms of city solicitors to open up *pro bono* units. By 1996, the Bar established a *Pro Bono* Unit of 650 barristers offering three days of unpaid work per year and the Law Society followed by establishing a solicitors' *Pro Bono* Group, prepared to offer some free advice to the unrepresented.

Marre Recommendations, 1988

1. To counteract low public awareness, lawyers should promote public education, public relations and informative advertising.
2. To overcome the public's fear of lawyers, they should develop an approachable, "shop-front" image, use interpreters and encourage ethnic minority practitioners.
3. Client dissatisfaction should be countered by reducing delay, using management training and keeping clients better informed.
4. Lawyers' services should be made more available by expanding the green form scheme to telephone and postal advice in rural areas, etc.

Civil Justice Review Recommendations, 1988

The outcomes are contained in square brackets.

1. Judicial interventionism where parties are unrepresented [C.L.S.A., s.6 provides rule-making power: see above].
2. A statutory right to lay representatives in minor county court cases [C.L.S.A. s.11].
3. Redesigning of explanatory leaflets. [New leaflets have been given the "crystal award" for clarity, by the Plain English Campaign.]
4. More assistance from court staff.
5. Closer links between courts and advice agencies.
6. Experiments with evening and written adjudications.
7. Reconsideration of conditional fees. [These were permitted, from 1995.]

Heilbron Report Recommendations, 1993

1. An ethos of public service should be revived among court officials. They should be more helpful to litigants in person.

2. Public facilities at court centres should be improved and procedure massively simplified.
3. A.D.R. should be directed and encouraged by courts. Lawyers should be trained in A.D.R.

Striking the Balance, 1996

This White Paper set out the Conservative Government's plans for reforming the funding and delivery of legal aid. As the new Labour Government will be finalising its plans in 1997–1998, students should concentrate on these as a predictor of a new legislative framework. The 1996 document becomes a matter of academic interest and a statement of the opposition view on legal aid.

Lord Mackay had proposed introducing pre-determined budgets for criminal, family and civil legal aid, which would be distributed via regional budgets, according to a formula devised by the Legal Aid Board. Expenditure would be targeted on priority areas. Most legal services would be provided through contracts with the Legal Aid Board.

Access to Justice, "the Woolf Report" 1996

Lord Woolf sees any review of legal aid funding as essentially linked to his proposals to reform access to civil justice and the new Government has accepted this in conducting a joint review in 1997–1998. He considers his proposed reforms will be more effective if:

- legal aid is available for A.D.R. for in-court advice services and for solicitors and barristers providing legal services to litigants conducting their own cases on the fast track;
- the Board's decisions take account of the court's allocation of a case to the appropriate track;
- and legal aid reforms recognise the importance of ensuring the survival of small firms of solicitors, especially in remote areas.

Labour's Plans on Legal Aid and Legal Services, 1995–1998

Labour's 1995 policy document, *Access to Justice*, was reaffirmed and added to by Lord Irvine L.C. in a speech to the Law Society in October 1997. Students should watch out for consultation papers, then a White Paper, likely to appear in 1998–1999 and

legislation in 1998–1999. Here is a summary of Labour's proposals to date (February, 1998):

- A community legal service will be created, to distribute the
  entire legal aid budget on a regional basis, co-ordinated by
  existing regional legal aid board offices. Each regional office
  will carry out a number of core functions:
  - assessing the legal needs of its area, including the need
    for A.D.R;
  - drawing up a detailed strategy to meet those needs in con-
    sultation with local authorities and new advisory regional
    legal services committees;
  - agreeing priorities for legal services with the help of legal
    services committees chosen to be representative of their
    community;
  - ensuring access to high quality legal representation
    through local private practice lawyers, CABx, law centres
    and other advice units "in order to create a comprehen-
    sive, nationwide, network of outlets for legal services";
  - promoting public legal education and preventative work;
    expanding vocational training for solicitors within law
    centres and advice agencies;
  - monitoring the quality of local legal provision.
- A.D.R. must be expanded.
- Tribunals should be easily accessible, informal, speedy and
  inexpensive. The lay element should be increased and the aim
  will be to reduce the need for legal representation.
- The Council on Tribunals' jurisdiction should be extended to
  supervising A.D.R.
- Resources will be transferred from ligation to mediation.
- The LCD may be restructured.
- Each region will have a body modelled on the NW Legal Services Committee, consisting of volunteers from court service
  officials, lawyers, local authority and consumer representatives. They may recommend research and reform to the LCD.
- Public legal education will promote awareness of citizens'
  rights and responsibilities, through schools, advice centres,
  libraries and courtrooms and all new Bills will include a clear
  statement of their policy objectives.
- Under used space in courts will be used to make legal advice
  and information available to all citizens.
- Information technology will be used to empower individuals to
  undertake the initial stages of their cases themselves.

- Multi-party actions will be permitted to enforce group rights on product liability, environmental damage and landlord and tenant cases.
- Franchising will play a key role, with more stringent and sophisticated quality control standards.
- Direct access to the Bar will be permitted, as will multi-disciplinary partnerships. Lawyers' restrictive practices will be scrutinised.
- Legal aid work will eventually be restricted to those with a fixed contract with the Legal Aid Board. Legislation will be needed for contracting out. Contracting will be extended to criminal legal aid.
- The merits test for civil legal aid will require a 75 per cent likelihood of success, except in public interest cases and those involving points of law.
- Conditional fees will be extended to the maximum possible, replacing legal aid in most claims for money or damages. Legal aid will remain available for family cases, care of children, judicial review and threats of homelessness.
- Consultations on these last three will take place in 1998 and a LCD project team will develop and carry forward detailed plans.

"Legal aid must be re-focused. It must be made a tool to promote access to justice for the needy – not be seen by the public as basically a means of keeping lawyers in business." (Lord Irvine L.C., October 1997).

APPEALS

Criminal Appeals

Appeals from the Magistrates' Court.

1. Appeals to the Crown Court. A defendant may appeal, as of right, on fact or law and against sentence and/or conviction. The appeal is a complete rehearing by a circuit judge and two to four magistrates.

The Crown Court may:

   (i)   correct any mistake in the order or judgment,
   (ii) confirm, reverse or vary the decision,
   (iii) remit the matter, with their opinion, to the magistrates,
   (iv) make any order they think just and exercise any power of

the magistrates' court. Thus, they may increase sentence, within the magistrates' maxima.

2. Appeals to the High Court by way of case stated. Any prosecutor or defendant, aggrieved by the magistrates' decision, may, if they consider it wrong in law or in excess of jurisdiction, apply to the magistrates to state a case for the opinion of the High Court.

The stated case is a statement of reasons for the decision drafted by the magistrates' clerk.

These appeals are heard by the Divisional Court of the QBD who may:

 (i)   reverse, affirm or amend the decision;
 (ii) remit it to the magistrates, with an opinion;
 (iii) make such other orders as they think fit, including directing the magistrates to convict or acquit. (**Note**: this is the only instance where a prosecutor can appeal to reverse an acquittal.)

Appeals from the Crown Court to the Court of Appeal (Criminal Division).

1. Appeal against conviction. Under the Criminal Appeal Act 1995, s.1, the convicted defendant may appeal if he has either a certificate from the trial judge that the case is fit for appeal or if leave of the Court of Appeal is obtained. Single High Court judges consider written applications for leave. Applicants have around a 25 per cent chance of success. Where leave is refused, the judge may order that time spent in custody after lodging the appeal should not count towards sentence. This is to discourage frivolous appeals, which burden the lists and delay meritorious appeals.

The Court of Appeals's powers are set out in the Criminal Appeal Act 1968, which has been substantially amended by the Criminal Appeal Act 1995. I will set out the amended version of the 1968 Act and then explain the background to the 1995 Act.

The Power of the Court of Appeal to Admit Fresh Evidence.

Under section 23(1) and (3) of the 1968 Act, as amended by the 1995 Act, the CA *may*, "if they think it necessary or expedient in the interests of justice"

(a) order the production of any document, exhibit or other thing connected with the proceedings;

(b) order the examination of any witness who would have been a compellable witness at the trial, whether or not he or she was called; and

(c) receive any evidence which was not adduced in the proceedings from which the appeal lies.

In considering in whether to receive evidence, the CA must have regard in particular to:

"(a) whether the evidence appears to the court to be capable of belief;

(b) whether it appears to the court that the evidence may afford any ground for allowing the appeal;

(c) whether the evidence would have been admissible in the proceedings from which the appeal lies on an issue which is the subject of the appeal; and

(d) whether there is a reasonable explanation for the failure to adduce the evidence in those proceedings" (1968 Act, s.23 (2), as substituted by section 4 of the 1995 Act).

Background

Under the old law (1968 Act until 1995), the CA had a duty to admit fresh evidence where it was not available at the original trial but a wider power to admit it "if they think it necessary or expedient in the interests of justice" (1968 Act, s.23). Several points arise:

(a) The Court of Appeal's strict approach was shown by these cases:

R. v. Flower (CA, 1965). Widgery J. said it was the duty of the court to consider and assess the reliability of witnesses and the court could then take one of three views:

(i) If satisfied that the fresh evidence was true and conclusive, the court would normally quash the conviction but, if not conclusive, order a retrial.

(ii) If not satisfied that the fresh evidence is true but nevertheless thinks it might be acceptable to a jury, the court would normally order a retrial.

(iii) If they disbelieve the evidence, they will disregard it;

but in *Stafford v. D.P.P.* (HL 1974) Viscount Dilhorne added that, if the court was satisfied that there was no reasonable doubt about the guilt of the accused, the conviction should not be quashed even though the jury might have come to a different view. The court was not bound to ask whether the evidence might have led to the jury returning a verdict of not guilty.

(b) This approach was criticised by Lord Devlin, who argued it was wrong, in principle, for judges rather than juries to decide whether the appellant was guilty. Where fresh evidence *could* have made a difference, the proper course would be for the court to order a new trial. The first verdict should be regarded as unsatisfactory simply because the original jury did not see all the evidence.

(c) The reluctance of the Court of Appeal to admit fresh evidence was repeatedly criticised by the pressure group, *Justice* and by the producers of the television series *Rough Justice* and authors of the book of the same name, all of which focused on alleged miscarriages of justice which resulted in wrongful imprisonment.

The cases they highlighted and similar, highly publicised ones showed that the Court of Appeal required a particular type of explanation why evidence was not called at the time of trial, such as that it was *not available*. If it was available but simply not called, owing to, say, defence lawyers' negligence, prosecution's obstructiveness or a shortfall of legal aid, then this apparently would not suffice as an explanation acceptable to the Court of Appeal. In many of these cases it took a "trial by television" and a reference by the Home Secretary to re-open the case. It appears, then, that the Court of Appeal was restricting its open *discretion* under the 1968 Act, s.23(1) and (3) by the criteria of s.23(2) (see above) which invoke the *duty* to admit fresh evidence. It was thus alleged to be perpetrating injustices by an over-reluctance to operate its discretion.

As public concern about miscarriages of justice reached a crescendo in the early 1980s, the House of Commons Home Affairs Committee produced a report entitled *Miscarriages of Justice* (see below). In its White Paper reply, the Government gave the following reassurance:

"The Lord Chief Justice . . . sees room for the Court to be more ready to exercise its own powers to receive evidence or, where appropriate and practicable, to order a retrial . . . The Lord Chief Justice has confirmed that the Court of Appeal is very ready to use its discretion to admit new evidence, under section 23 of the Criminal Appeal Act 1968, when the interests of justice so require."

Nevertheless, *Justice* reported, in its 1989 publication *Miscarriages of Justice*, that practice had not noticeably changed. The Royal Commission on Criminal Justice, in 1993 again urged the CA to take a broad approach to the question whether fresh evidence was available at the time of the trial and, if it were, to the explanation why it was not adduced or why a witness had changed her story. The test for receiving fresh evidence should be whether it was "capable of belief." In fresh evidence cases, the CA should order a retrial unless impracticable, in which case they should decide the case themselves.

In their responding 1994 consultation paper, the Home Office broadly agreed but thought the CA's power to exclude fresh evidence should be preserved, in cases where there was no reasonable explanation for the failure to produce it at trial. As you can see, this is satisfied in the Act by the use of the word *may* in conjunction with their power to have regard to the explanation offered.

Grounds for Allowing and Dismissing Appeals. Section 2 of the Criminal Appeal Act 1968, as amended by the 1995 Act, now provides that:

"Subject to the provisions of this Act, the Court of Appeal
(a) shall allow an appeal against conviction if they think that the conviction is unsafe; and
(b) shall dismiss such an appeal in any other case."

Background. Under the un-amended Act, the Court had the power to allow an appeal if they thought a jury's verdict "unsafe or unsatisfactory" or that there was an error of law or material irregularity in the course of the trial. Section 2 included a very important "proviso" which meant that the Court could dismiss an appeal where, despite finding that something had gone wrong at the trial, they thought the defendant was, nevertheless, really guilty so that "no miscarriage of justice has actually occurred". The CA had been criticised for too readily using the proviso to uphold convictions where something had gone seriously wrong at the trial.

The R.C.C.J. recommended that section 2(1) of the 1968 Act should be redrafted. They considered that the grounds overlapped and that there was confusion over the proviso. The grounds, they recommended, should be replaced by a single broad ground, giving the CA power to rule in any case where it felt a conviction "is or may be unsafe." The proviso would be redundant if the CA simply dismissed an appeal where they found an error had not rendered a conviction unsafe or ordered a retrial in those cases where it considered a conviction may be unsafe. This power would be exercisable regardless of there being no fresh evidence, no error in law and no material irregularity.

The CA should have an additional power to refer cases that require further investigation to a new body to be responsible for investigating alleged miscarriages of justice.

The Government broadly agreed with these proposals in its 1994 Home Office consultation paper, *Criminal Appeals and the Establishment of A Criminal Cases Review Authority* but notice that the CA now has to be satisfied that the verdict *is* unsafe. The Commission's words "or may be" have not been included in the section. Critics have said that this is too restrictive on the CA's powers. Although the proviso is now abolished, the court's new powers may have the same effect.

As well as the power to quash a conviction, the Court also has the power to order a retrial (discussed below) or convict for an alternative offence, or substitute a verdict of insanity or unfitness to plead.

The Court of Appeal's attitude towards its powers. Generally speaking, the CA was criticised for placing too restrictive an interpretation on its already limited powers. Prior to 1995, section 2 had been interpreted by Widgery L.J. in *R. v. Cooper* (CA, 1969) as requiring the CA judges to ask themselves the substantive question "whether there is not some lurking doubt in our minds, which makes us wonder whether an injustice has been done." The R.C.C.J. thought the Court should be less reluctant to use its powers to overturn jury verdicts but the Home Secretary and the judges, at the time of the passage of the 1995 Act, said the new version of section 2 simply restates the Court's previous practice. The main reason why the CA is so reluctant to overturn a conviction by a jury is that, unlike the jury, they have not seen the witnesses and evidence first-hand. Further, they tend to revere the primacy of the jury, as the quotation below illustrates.

It is important to understand that the CA does not provide a rehearing in criminal cases, unlike an appeal from a magistrates' court to the Crown Court. The limited powers of the CA were spelled out in the successful appeal of the Birmingham Six, in 1991,

R. v. McIlkenny and ors, in a judgment read out by the judges in turn:

> "Nothing in s.2 of the Act, or anywhere else obliges or entitles us to say whether we think that the appellant is innocent. This is a point of great constitutional importance. The task of deciding whether a man is innocent or guilty falls on the jury. We are concerned solely with the question whether the verdict of the jury can stand.
>
> Rightly or wrongly (we think rightly) trial by jury is the foundation of our criminal justice system. ... The primacy of the jury in the criminal justice system is well illustrated by the difference between the Criminal and Civil Divisions of the Court of Appeal. ... A civil appeal is by way of rehearing of the whole case. So the court is concerned with fact as well as law. ... It follows that in a civil case the Court of Appeal may take a different view of the facts from the court below. In a criminal case this is not possible ... the Criminal Division is perhaps more accurately described as a court of review."

The Power to order retrials. The 1968 Act, s.7, as amended by the Criminal Justice Act 1988, provides that, where the CA allows an appeal against convinction, it may order that the appellant be retried where it appears that this is required in the interests of justice.

Background. Prior to the 1988 amendment, the CA could only order a retrial where it had admitted fresh evidence. Some critics say the amendment does not go far enough and that the CA should have been given a wider power, as exists in Scotland.

Justice. considered whether the Court of Appeal should have unlimited power to order retrials, following appeals from conviction. They found opinions so divided that they published both sides' views, which can be summarised as follows:

Anti-retrials

(a) Absence of a general power of retrial ensures the accused cannot be subjected to a second ordeal.
(b) Statistics show a new general power would be used infrequently.
(c) Most cases where the Court of Appeal has complained of a lack of power to order retrial are cases where they have allowed an appeal. There is no reason why the judicial system should be allowed a second attempt to provide a fair trial.

(d) There is no evidence that retrial would replace some dismissals of appeal.

(e) There are real doubts as to the fairness of a second trial. The second jury may well now know of the defendant's record and have noted other adverse publicity, as well as knowing that the defendant has been convicted.

(f) Practitioners dislike new trials because the evidence is stale and cross-examination cannot be successful.

(g) Experience from abroad is adverse.

(h) Those pro-retrial recommend only one retrial. There can be no logical reason for this so they impliedly admit to the oppressiveness of retrial.

Pro-retrials

(a) A general power to order retrial would assist in acquitting the innocent and convicting the guilty.

(b) The majority of wrongful convictions result from mistaken identify. This will not be quashed by the Court of Appeal but they might order retrials if they could.

As stated above, the 1988 Act extends the power of retrial. A useful analysis is made by Alldridge [1987] N.L.J. 1189.

The R.C.C.J. favoured retrials where possible. In non-fresh evidence cases, where a retrial was desirable but impracticable, the CA, they recommended, should automatically allow an appeal. In fresh evidence cases, they should decide the appeal themselves only if a retrial were impracticable. The Home Office, in its response, disagreed with the first recommendation, preferring that the CA decide these cases itself.

Appeals against Sentence. The defendant may appeal from the Crown Court to the CA, who may substitute any other sentence or order within the powers of the Crown Court, provided it is not more severe than originally. The Criminal Justice Act 1988, s. 36 gives the Attorney-General a prosecutorial power to refer any "unduly lenient" Crown Court sentence to the CA, who then have the power to increase it. The Attorney may then refer any such decision of the CA to the House of Lords.

Attorney-General's References. The Attorney may, under the Criminal Justice Act 1972, refer an appeal, following an acquittal, to the CA and HL, on behalf of the prosecution. The appeal court simply clarifies the law, leaving the acquittal untouched.

Appeals to the House of Lords.

1. Appeals from the High Court ("leapfrog" appeals). Either prosecutor or defendant may appeal, with leave, to the House of Lords, from an appeal hearing in the Divisional Court, on a point of law of general public importance. (Administration of Justice Act 1960.)

2. Appeals from the Court of Appeal. Either prosecutor or defendant may appeal, provided the Court of Appeal certifies that a point of law of general public importance is involved and that either court considers that the point should be considered by the House and grants leave. The House, in disposing of the appeal, may exercise any of the powers of the Court of Appeal, or remit the case to it. (Criminal Appeal Act 1968.)

The Post Appeal Stage: Re-examining Alleged Miscarriages of Justice.

Where a person thinks he has been wrongly convicted by a jury or magistrates and he has lost an appeal or been refused leave to appeal, he may now seek the assistance of the newly created Criminal Cases Review Commission or somebody else may petition them on his behalf. (Judging from the past, this is likely to be an M.P. or a campaigning group, or an organisation such as *Justice*). It was created by Part II of the 1995 Act and started work in 1997. It is a body corporate, independent of the Crown. Its 11 members are appointed for terms of five years. At least one third must be legally qualified. The Commission is empowered to refer Crown Court convictions and sentences to the Court of Appeal and summary convictions and sentences to the Crown Court. The Commission must "consider that there is a real possibility that the conviction, verdict, finding or sentence would not be upheld, were the reference to be made" because of argument or evidence not raised earlier. These conditions appear rather restrictive but these are followed by a broad power to make a reference "if it appears to the Commission that there are exceptional circumstances which justify making it."

The Commission may be directed by the Court of Appeal to investigate a case and may be asked by the Home Secretary to consider a matter arising in his consideration of whether to exercise the prerogative of mercy. The Commission has powers to obtain documents and may direct investigations by police officers or another public body.

Although the Commission is a welcome replacement for the former arrangements for investigating miscarriages of justice, the statute has been criticised for not providing the body with independent investigators and concern has been expressed that its first chairman is a senior freemason.

Background. Prior to 1995, the Home Secretary had both a prerogative power of mercy, which he retains, and a statutory power, under section 17 of the 1968 Act, to refer cases to the CA.

Constitutionally, the Home Secretary has always used the prerogative to pardon sparingly, so as not to invoke the criticism of over-interference of the executive in the judicial function and because of the notion that the jury's verdict is sacrosanct. The House of Commons Home Affairs Committee complained in 1981 that the prerogative was used reluctantly, that decisions of vital importance to the liberty of the individual were taken anonymously by civil servants, after unexplained delays and with no reasons given for a complainant's rejection. They recommended an independent review body to advise on the exercise of the prerogative, rendering the use of referrals under section 17 redundant. In its White Paper reply, however, the Government rejected these proposals, on the constitutional grounds mentioned above but gave the assurance that the Home Secretary would be more ready to refer cases to the Court of Appeal and that Home Office procedures in dealing with petitions for the prerogative would be reviewed. In its 1989 publication, *Miscarriages of Justice*, however (see below), *Justice* reported that there had been fewer references per year since this assurance was given, not more.

The R.C.C.J. proposed that the Home Secretary's power under section 17 be replaced by a new authority, along the lines of that now created. The Home Office responded, in a 1994 consultation paper, expanding on the Royal Commission's recommendations.

They drew attention to the difficult constitutional issues involved in establishing the relationship between the Authority and the Court of Appeal, such as the need to prevent the Authority from usurping the courts's functions.

The royal prerogative of mercy. The prerogative of mercy is the power to pardon convicted individuals as part of the residuary royal prerogative, exercised by the Crown on the advice of the Home Secretary, effectively, by civil servants. The prerogative is exercised in three ways:

(a) A free pardon: quashing and expunging a conviction.
(b) A conditional pardon: excusing or varying the conviction, subject to conditions, *e.g.* by commuting sentences.
(c) Remission of a sentence.

General Background to the Criminal Appeal Act 1995— Widespread Concern Over Miscarriages of Justice

The most famous miscarriages of justice in modern times were the cases of the Guildford Four and the Birmingham Six. The R.C.C.J. was established on the day the latter were released, in 1991, to investigate the criminal justice process. Concerns had, however, been raised for decades beforehand, over individuals who had allegedly been wrongfully imprisoned. Television programmes such as *Rough Justice* had alerted the public to the inadequacy of the appeal and post-appeal procedures. These are probably best summarised in a *Justice* Report, *Miscarriages of Justice*, 1989 known as *The Waller Report*. It is well worth reading and, below, I list the causes of injustice identified by their report, explaining, in square brackets, how these were later manifested in these famous cases:

Pre-Trial

a. Poor work by defence lawyers.
b. Cases involving poor police investigation and/or police misconduct. [The stories behind the Guildford Four and Birmingham Six involve a sad litany of police corruption, notably of police brutality inducing false confessions.] The Report recites psychiatric research which gives a fascinating insight into why people confess to crimes they did not commit.

Trial

c. Poor work by defence counsel: late briefs, bad trial tactics and failure to call witnesses.
d. Underhand tactics by the prosecution. [In the Guildford Four case, it was alleged that the police realised, early on, that they

might not have caught the right people but they suppressed evidence in favour of the defence, such as an interview with an alibi witness.]

e. Poor summing up by the judge. [In the Guildford Four case, the summing up by the trial judge was acknowledged by the Court of Appeal to be faulty but they did not consider it sufficient reason to allow leave to appeal. As for the Birmingham Six, the summing up by their trial judge (who later became a Law Lord) went overboard in indicating a guilty verdict.]

Appeal

f. Bad advice on appeal.
g. The majority of appeals are concerned with legal technicalities, not the guilt or innocence of the accused.
h. A reluctance to interfere with the trial verdict. [In the Birmingham Six case, the Court of Appeal, headed by Lord Lane C.J., which heard the Six's 1987 appeal, was very heavily criticised for its refusal to overturn the jury's verdict, despite new evidence casting serious doubt on the convictions.]

Post-Appeal

i. The desire of the Home Secretary, as part of the executive, not to be seen to be interfering with the work of the courts leads him to ignore errors under a. to g. [By the time the Home Secretary had referred the Birmingham Six's appeal back to the Court of Appeal, the case had already been the subject of a book and a T.V. drama documentary and opinion polls showed that most Americans, including President Bush and most Irish people, including their Prime Minister, assumed the Six to be innocent.]

j. Inadequate re-investigation by the police. [The police were criticised for taking two years to investigate the Guildford Four's convictions.]

Additionally, the above cases highlighted specific weaknesses in the system:

k. Inefficiency in forensic science services and inadequate services for the defence, as emphasised by the May inquiry into the Guildford and Maguire cases.

l. Inadequate safeguards for defendants held under the Prevention of Terrorism Act. **Note**: many commentators have said the injustices occurring in the Irish cases could not now be repeated, because of PACE. This is erroneous. Today, suspected terrorists are still held under the PTA.

m. The danger of allowing the jury to convict on uncorroborated confession evidence.

n. Over-anxiety on the part of the police to secure a conviction, including a preparedness to fabricate evidence, in cases where there is a public outcry against the perpetrators. All these cases involve Irish or black defendants.

o. Over-willingness in certain Court of Appeal judges to believe prosecution evidence, probably caused by the fact that the majority of them are recruited from prosecuting counsel.

p. Limited powers of the Court of Appeal: an inability to provide a full rehearing.

They drew attention to the difficult constitutional issues involved in establishing the relationship between the Authority and the Court of Appeal, such as the need to prevent the Authority from usurping the courts' functions.

Civil Appeals

Appeals from Magistrates' Courts.

1. Appeals to the Crown Court. As in criminal cases, appeal lies to the Crown Court, *e.g.* in licensing cases.

2. Appeals to the High Court by way of case stated, to the Queen's Bench Division and the Family Division (Divisional Courts).

3. Appeals to the High Court in family cases. In certain family matters, appeal lies on fact or law to the Divisional Court of the Family Division. The Court may substitute any order made by the magistrates or remit for rehearing.

Appeals from the County Court to the Court of Appeal (Civil Division).

Appeal lies to the Court of Appeal generally, as of right on fact or law. Leave must be obtained in certain classes of case prescribed by Rules of the Supreme Court (C.L.S.A., s.7). There is a list of statutory exceptions, such as appeal where the parties have agreed in writing that the judges's decision shall be final. In other cases, leave is needed, such as where the claim is under £5,000 or, in property cases, under £15,000.

Appeals lie from district judge's decision to a circuit judge.

Appeals from the High Court to the Court of Appeal (Civil Division).

Again, C.L.S.A., s.7 (as above). Where leave is needed it must be sought first from the High Court and thereafter may be sought from the Court of Appeal.

The mode of appeal is a "rehearing" but not a true rehearing. Rather, it involves the judges reading depositions of witnesses' evidence at trial. The court has power to draw new inferences from facts found.

The court must take account of any new authorities or material changes in fact since the trial. It also has the power to admit fresh evidence on "special grounds" (RSC Ord. 59). The criteria upon which fresh evidence may be admitted have been set out by Denning L.J. in *Ladd v. Marshall* (C.A. 1954).

The Court of Appeal is reluctant to overturn *findings of fact* by the trial judge in the same way that it is reluctant to overturn a jury's verdict in a criminal case (remember, a "lurking doubt" is the criterion for overturning a jury's verdict). The House of Lords has warned off the Court of Appeal from interfering, in cases such as the *S.S. Hontestroom v. S.S. Sagaporack* (HL 1929). Lord Summer said:

> "not to have seen the witnesses puts the appellate judges in a permanent position of disadvantage, as against the trial judge, and, unless it can be shown that he has failed to use or has palpably misused his advantage, the higher court ought not to take responsibility of reversing conclusions so arrived at, merely on the result of their own comparisons and criticisms of the witnesses and of their own view of the probability of the case. The course of the trial and the whole substance of the judgment must be looked at. . . ."

He then endorsed Lord Kingsdown in *The Julia* (PC 1860):

> "We must, in order to reverse, not merely entertain doubts whether the decision below is right, but be convinced that it is wrong."

This looks a more stringent test than the "lurking doubt" needed to overturn a jury's decision. The Court of Appeal is, however, much less reluctant to overturn *inferences from fact* by a trial judge (*e.g. Whitehouse v. Jordan* (CA 1981)).

The Court of Appeal will only overturn an award of damages where a judge has made a wholly erroneous estimate of the damage suffered. The C.L.S.A., s.8 introduced a power to make rules permitting the CA to substitute damages where an excessive or inadequate award has been made by a jury (*e.g.* those awarded against the publishers of *Private Eye* for defaming Sonia Sutcliffe, wife of "The Yorkshire Ripper").

As far as discretionary decisions are concerned, the appeal court will not interfere with the trial judge's decision unless the trial judge erred in law, was mistaken as to facts, took account of irrelevant matters, failed to exercise his discretion or acted in some other way wrongly, in principle.

Both the Court of Appeal and the High Court have the power to order a civil retrial (Supreme Court Act 1981), where fresh evidence is discovered, a witness confesses to having given false evidence, where the case has been misconducted by a judge or counsel, or where the trial is in some other way unfair. In relation to the rare cases where there has been a civil jury trial, a retrial may also be ordered after a misdirection, improper regulation of evidence or that the verdict was against the weight of evidence. The Court of Appeal must be satisfied of some "substantial wrong or miscarriage."

Appeals from the High Court to the House of Lords ("leapfrogging").

Certain rare appeals are allowed, with leave, direct from the High Court, by-passing the Court of Appeal, under the Administration of Justice Act 1969. The trial judge must be satisfied that a sufficient case for a "leap-frog" has been made out, that the parties consent and that these conditions are fulfilled:

(i) that a point of law of general public importance is involved; and
(ii) that it involves statutory construction or where the trial judge was bound by the Court of Appeal or House of Lords.

Appeals from the Court of Appeal to the House of Lords.

An appeal lies from any judgment of the Court of Appeal. An application for leave must be made first to the Court of Appeal and, if refused, may be made to the House of Lords.

Appeals are normally heard by five Law Lords. The parties must each lodge a printed "case," supposedly being a succinct statement of the arguments below and of the issues before the House. Theoretically, all Law Lords will have read this "case" and the judgments in the court below in advance of the hearing. This emphasis on written argument has been used to reduce oral argument before the House. Judgment is normally reserved and their Lordships' opinions delivered some days or weeks later. Any orders made are, technically, High Court orders, as the House has no machinery for enforcement.

References to the European Court of Justice

Article 177 EEC concerns references to the European Court of Justice by domestic courts of Member States:

"(1) The Court of Justice shall have jurisdiction to give preliminary rulings concerning:

(a) the interpretation of the Treaty;
(b) the validity and interpretation of acts of the institutions of the Community and of the ECB;
(c) the interpretation of the statutes of bodies established by an Act of the Council, where those statutes so provide.

(2) Where such a question is raised before any court or tribunal of a Member State, that court or tribunal may, if it considers that a decision on the question is necessary to enable it to give judgment, request the Court of Justice to give a ruling thereon.

(3) Where any such question is raised in a case pending before a court or tribunal of a Member State, against whose decisions there is no judicial remedy under national law, that court or tribunal shall bring the matter before the Court of Justice."

Points to note about Article 177 are these:

(a) Any judicial or quasi-judicial body may refer, however lowly. For instance, magistrates' courts and tribunals.
(b) The "question" may be raised by the parties or the court but only the court may make the reference.
(c) The ruling is *preliminary* only in the sense that the case then goes back to the original court for it to apply the law to the facts. Obviously, the ECJ's rulings on E.C. law, etc., are final.
(d) The ECJ will not answer hypothetical questions.

(e) Facts should normally be found before reference but there may be exceptional cases.

(f) The ECJ has accepted the doctrine of *acte clair*. This means that a point need not be referred if it is "reasonably clear and free from doubt."

(g) References under Article 177 are discretionary, except where there is no judicial remedy against the domestic court's decision. In that instance, an *obligation* to refer arises under Article 177(3).

---

6. EXAM TIPS, MODEL QUESTIONS AND ANSWER GUIDES

EXAM TIPS

Revision: How?

Start early in the year. You have a three month summer holiday, so use Easter to revise hard, otherwise you may waste the summer (or all next year!) revising for a resit. Draw up a revision timetable and stick to it. You will underestimate the time taken to revise. If your lecture notes and others are scrappy, you *may* find it helpful to make revision notes.

Revision: What?

You should aim to know the whole course fairly well and, as much of it as possible, in greater depth. *Question spotting* is very difficult in E.L.S., as there can be so many different permutations of topics, *e.g.* "the adversarial process" includes civil and criminal trial and pre-trial; legal profession might be combined with judiciary or with legal services, etc. It helps, however, to *know your own course*. Know the topics your course teachers have emphasised in *your year*. Topicality means past papers are, in some respects, unhelpful. Whereas in 1989, I set questions on the Civil Justice Review, the obvious topics of 1997 are the Labour Government's proposals on legal aid and civil justice (implementation of Woolf). Do *not* revise from notes for other courses and do not fool yourself that this *Nutshell* is anything but a revision aid, a comforter. It is not a substitute for having worked hard and, in this subject, *read widely*, throughout the year. Beware that it may omit things emphasised in *your* course, *e.g.* bail, family courts, Ministry of Justice.

Know the *approach* of your course, as well as its content, *e.g.* at Kingston, E.L.S. for law undergraduates is highly critical, sometimes political and always analytical and discursive, much more so than this *Nutshell*, but the ability to appreciate E.L.S. in the context of this approach comes from wide reading. E.L.S. for undergraduates in non-law courses and students on other courses, is usually much more factual, and a "tools for the trade" approach.

In the Exam

Organise your time. Every year I groan over a handful of 2A students who achieve 3rds or fails because they have answered two and a half or three questions instead of four. Think about it. If you answer three instead of four, you must achieve an *average* of 66 per cent in those three, just to attain an examination mark of 50 per cent (*just* a 2B). Divide the exam time by the number of answers required and force yourself to move on when time is up. Leave ample space between answers to add points, even in neat note form, to your earlier answers, if you can spare 10 minutes at the end. Lecturers always say and some students never seem to understand the simple point that it is much easier to gain 30 marks on answering a new question than to add 30 to a near-complete one. *Do not waffle. Write clearly.* Try rollerball or superior ballpoint. See which is quicker and neater. Fountain pens are too slow. Bad writing is *bound* to affect the markers, as they cannot get the "gist," the "flow" of an argument, even if they can slowly interpret it, word by word. If your handwriting is bad, get help urgently, in college or privately. *If English is not your first language* practise it by getting as much of your written English checked as you can persuade people to mark (on any topic). Again, if you need remedial help, your college may provide it. In the exam, you need time for mental translation. Time will be your enemy so make every word count. Waffle is even more dangerous for you than a native student.

Answer the question set. If you panic and mis-read a question on juries as one on magistrates, you may get 0. If you "write all you know" where a critical analysis or a particular approach is needed, you *may*, but only if you are lucky, scrape a pass, however detailed you are and however much you have learned. Plan and present your answer and *only* include that which is required. Do not be tempted to demonstrate knowledge just because you have revised it.

Be authoritative. The trouble with this subject is that every *Sun* reader has an opinion on the jury or the legal profession. You must substantiate your beliefs with fact and authoritative opinion. Most opinions have found written expression in some text, article or committee report, sometimes in many, but do not invent sources/ quotations. Your examiner will know better. Being authoritative comes from *wide reading*, not a *Nutshell*. *Be original*: very difficult but the more so the better. Reach your own *informed* opinions. Draw on your own observation of courts and tribunals. They provide hours of free entertainment on a wet Wednesday afternoon. Read a quality newspaper daily. Search for new commentaries and articles in law journals.

QUESTIONS AND ANSWERS

I thoroughly disapprove of model answers to questions on the English legal system for law undergraduates. The questions I set may be *very* different from those set in your course, so beware. I usually set questions which require the student to know the facts but, more importantly, to use imagination and express an informed, substantiated opinion. The concept of a "model" answer is nonsense and the danger of such "models" is that they may stifle imagination. I mark questions without a preconceived idea of "the" answer, although there may be only one legitimate set of parameters.

These are only my suggestions below. You can find different ways of arguing the same or evidence to argue the opposite. Do not be daunted. My opinion is worth no more than yours, provided yours is relevant and *substantiated*.

QUESTION 1

Comment critically on the use of lay people as decision makers in the English legal system.

Answer Notes

This question is so wide it provides ample scope but could give you enough rope to hang yourself, if you fail to identify what is required. "Lay people" includes magistrates *and* juries *plus* tribunal members and arbitrators. "Decision makers" excludes expert witnesses. Comment critically does not mean criticise any more or less than a theatre critic. If you think their use should be protected then say so and why. "The use" suggests non-use. If not used, what is the alternative? Professionals?

Use of lay justices. Cheap. Unique. The system would collapse without them. Pros and cons of lay justices or stipendiaries. Obvious advantages of having "ordinary people" judge or sentence most petty offenders and hear family and juvenile cases but are they "ordinary people?" Problems of achieving a balanced bench, socially, politically, occupationally, let alone in intelligence. Use of lay people O.K. if they are trained to understand their job without over-training and if not dominated by the professionals in court, especially clerks.

Use of jurors. Traditional civil libertarian support. Democracy, etc. Devlin, Blackstone BUT cons.: decline in jury use in civil cases due to lack of confidence (reasons) and very few criminal cases use jury trial so how can it be a significant guardian of civil liberties, etc.? Roskill report suggested abolition in fraud cases. Not followed but thin end of the wedge? Like magistrates, advantage is supposed to be trial by representatives of the man in the street. Randomness and representativeness eroded by statute, excuses, vetting.

Use of tribunal panel and arbitrators. Advantage: expertise and, in some tribunals, *e.g.* industrial, a balanced panel must instil some confidence. O.K. so long as sufficient law injected by lawyer chairman.

Alternatives. Professional judges. Pros and cons. Decide for yourself.

QUESTION 2

Is the system of selection and training of the judiciary likely to produce judges fitted to perform their constitutional role as independent, impartial arbiters?

Answer Notes

Expand on what you understand by "constitutional role" and "independence," etc. Political? Aloof from corruption and outside influences? Define impartial. Analyse system of appointment, selection and training in the light of all this. Make only relevant points and link them to the question, continually.

Selection. Predominantly from Bar, especially superior judiciary. No career judiciary in England, as in Europe, so circuit judges cannot necessarily expect promotion to High Court. Bar elitist, expensive to enter. Difficult to find a tenancy. Anachronistic rules mark it out from solicitors/public. Cloistered socialisation. High Court judges selected from small number of eligible Q.C.s. Hardly surprising most superior judges come from higher social classes, public school and Oxbridge. Now, throughout 1990s, Lord Chancellor has been criticised for recruitment policies that are racist, sexist and exclude solicitors. How can this narrow social background fit them for impartially judging all social classes and understanding the evidence before them? The C.L.S.A. obviously gives scope for more solicitor appointments. Will this have any impact? What do *you* think? Do you have any alternatives? Would *Justice*'s suggestion of appointing academics help? Would a career judiciary help?

Selection by Lord Chancellor, political appointee. Dubious, constitutionally, as a breach of separation of powers. Open to accusations of political bias, even if recent Lord Chancellors have acted independently. The E.L.S. is elsewhere concerned with appearances: "justice should be seen to be done." Few judges now are ex-M.P.s, as at the turn of the century, however.

Even if judges are party politically independent, they are still likely to hold conservative, established views because they are selected by Lord Chancellor and senior civil servants; average age on appointment is high. History of judicial activity in administrative law, labour law, civil liberties, as recounted by Griffith. Thus, even if party politically impartial, they come from a limited social/political group. Will the new Labour Government eventually create a Judicial Appointments Commission? If so, how would you like it to be consituted? What criteria should it use for selecting judges?

Alternatives? *Justice* (1992) suggested a Judicial Appointments Commission. Career judiciary? Use your imagination.

Training. Precious little. Experience on the job. Otherwise experience as an advocate, the antithesis of training. *Justice* report and judicial studies working party said they should be trained. On what? Use your imagination, *e.g.* sociology, courtroom psychology, criminology, penology, even law, for those from the specialist Bar. Civil Justice Review recommended a more interventionist judicial role so should be training in case management techniques. Also, if they are to be more interventionist in helping unrepresented parties in the lower courts, they need training for this too. Could they, conceivably, be trained to be impartial?

The Court Structure

European Court of Justice

Applications for preliminary rulings (Art. 177) actions against Member States, etc

15 judges advised by 9 advocates-general

Leapfrog appeals – law only, point of general public importance; consent of HL, HC and parties

House of Lords

Appeals from Court of Appeal and High Court, Scotland and Northern Ireland

Lord Chancellor, Lords of Appeal in Ordinary. Minimum 3

Privy Council

Appeals from the Commonwealth, G.M.C. etc.

Lord President, Lord Chancellor, Privy Councillors (Lords of Appeal) etc.

Mostly appeals of general public importance – leave needed

Court of Appeal

Civil Division	**Criminal Division**
Appeals from the High Court and county courts	Appeals from the Crown Court and QBD
M.R. and Lord Justices of Appeal	**L.C.J., Lords Justices od Appeal and High Court Judges**

appeals on law / fact / sentence

appeals on law – leave sometimes needed

High Court

Chancery Division	**Family Division**	**Queen's Bench Division**
Tax, probate, bankruptcy, property, trusts, Patents Court, Companies Court	Divorce, matrimonial property, proceedings under the Children Act	Contract, Tort etc. Admiralty Court, Commercial Court
V.C and High Court Judges	**President and High Court Judges**	**L.C.J. and High Court Judges**
Divisional Court	**Divisional Court**	**Divisional Court**
Appeals in bankruptcy	Appeals from magistrates' courts	Appeals by case stated from Crown Court and magistrates' courts. Supervisory jurisdiction.

rare appeals

appeals

County Court

Most actions below £25,000. Equity and probate – £30,000. Personal injury actions – £50,000. Small claims £3,000. Actions £25,000–£50,000 of low complexity, importance and substance. Similar actions over £50,000 transferred by H.C. Family proceedings.

Circuit Judges and District Judges

Magistrates' Court

Civil – family proceedings. Criminal – Trial of summary offences and triable either way: £5,000/6 months. Youth Court

2 or 3 lay justices or 1 stipendiary, advised by a justices' clerk or court clerk

Crown Court

Jury trials of indictable offences and offences triable either way; appeals from magistrates' courts. Divided into 3 tiers

High Court Judges, Circuit Judges, Recorders, Magistrates

OTHER COURTS

"Court of Protection": an Office" where Chancery judges manage property of the mentally ill.

Coroners' Courts: Coroner and jury deal with sudden deaths

Official Referees' Court: Circuit judges hear complex High Court cases, mainly building contracts.

Restrictive Practices Court: Puisne judges and lay people hear restrictive practices and fair trading cases.

Employment Appeals Tribunal: Appeals from industrial tribunals.

appeals

INDEX